LEGACY

PRINCIPLED MANAGEMENT

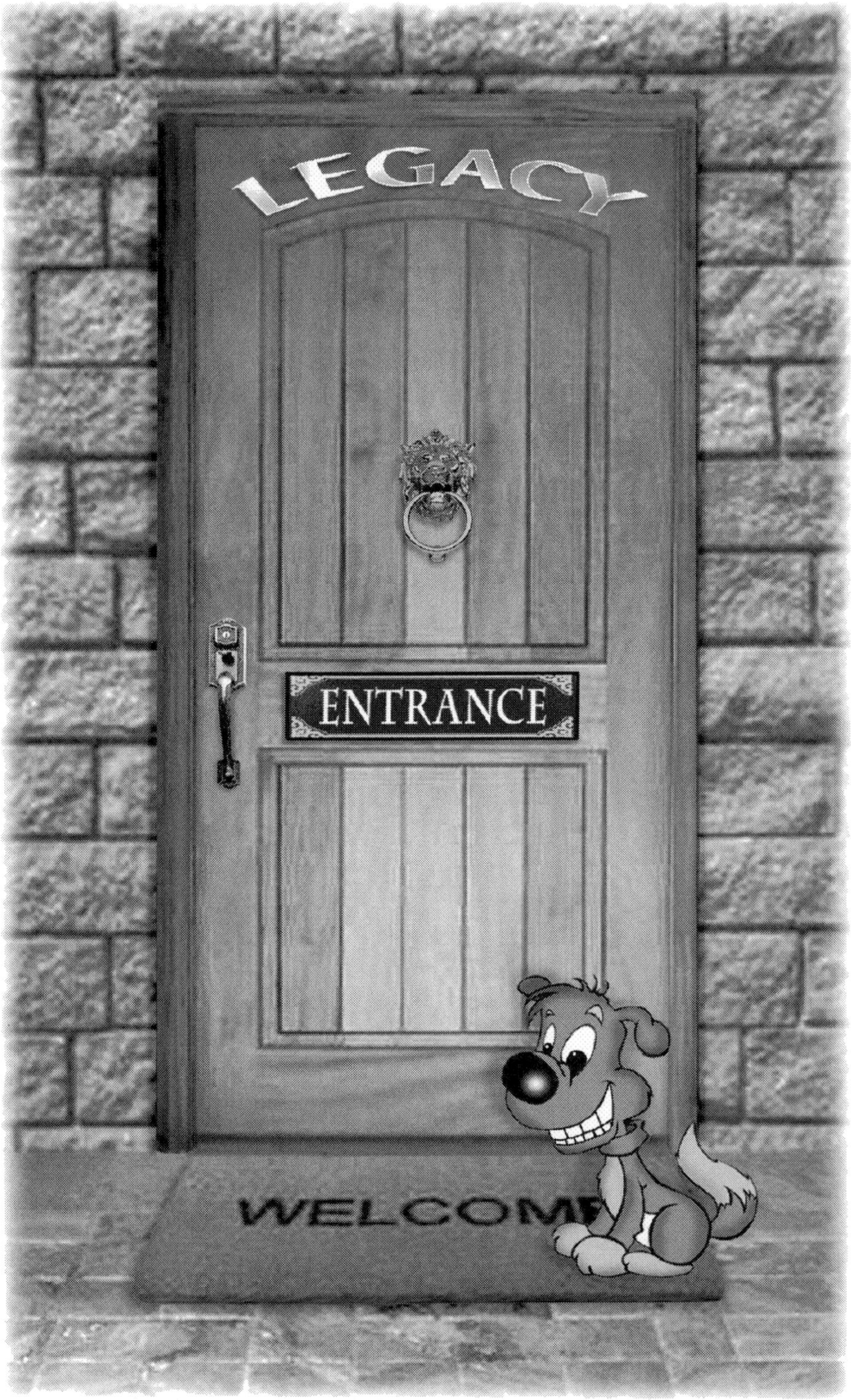
LEGACY
ENTRANCE
WELCOME

You are a business leader... What do you want your legacy to be?

In <u>Legacy - Principled Management</u>, you will see your career in a very different light - as a servant-leader, impacting the well-being of all those you encounter.

As we examine the seven foundational building blocks of business, I will share valuable business systems and timeless management principles gleaned from Scripture. These principles, when integrated with your own company values, can produce beneficial and lasting results.

In <u>Legacy - Principled Management</u>, you will learn how to inspire purpose into your management team's performance. You will learn to connect recognition and rewards for every employee to the customer-focused mission of your company. Most importantly, you will learn principles - like the <u>Principle of Interdependency</u> and the <u>Principle of Peace</u> that will serve you well throughout your life, whether personally or in business.

In the Prologue, as well as in the introduction to each chapter, I have addressed my own children and grandchildren. Whatever principles they may choose to assimilate into their own lives from this collection of my experiences will truly be a most rewarding legacy. And if these principles should prove beneficial to an even wider circle of readers than my own family, I will consider that an added blessing.

Linc Duncanson

Page design and layout, including all cartoons, graphics, and other artwork were created exclusively for *Legacy - Principled Management* by Cliff Bjork

Table of Contents

Prologue.............A Message from Dad

Chapter 1............What You Should Know About Yourself................. 1
- Your Personal Values and Life Purpose (2)
- Your Personal Assessment (10)
  - ✓ Your Strengths – How You Can Help Others
  - ✓ Your Weaknesses – How Others Can Help You
  - ✓ Your Change Plan – The Wheel of Life
  - ✓ Keeping Yourself Grounded – Keeping in Balance
- Your Personal Discipline (17)

Chapter 2............Management Philosophy: 19
What is Principled Management?

Chapter 3............Vision, Mission & Values 23

Chapter 4............Strategic Customer-Focused Business Plan 37

Chapter 5............Strategic Marketing & Sales Plan 45
- The Difference Between "**Big M**" and "small m" Marketing (47)
- Marketing Models (49)
- Distinctive Competencies (52)
- A Simple Marketing Approach That Works (53)
- Building Your Strategic Sales Plan From Your Strategic Marketing Plan (56)
- Customer Relationship Management (60)
- Measuring the Immeasurable – Customer Satisfaction (62)

Chapter 6............Information & Communications Systems............ 65

Chapter 7............Human Resources Plan.. 69

Chapter 8............Critical Business Systems..................................... 83

Chapter 9............Performance Management System 87

Chapter 10..........Incentive Compensation....................................... 93

Chapter 11..........Principles... 103

- Principle of "Family" (104)
- Principle of Interdependency (108)
- Principle of Respect (110)
- Principle: Don't Mess with a Person's Name or His Pay (112)
- Principle of Contribution-Based Pay (113)
- Principle of Honesty (115)
- Principle of Confrontation (116)
- Principle of "Values in Action" (117)
- Principle of Owning Problems (118)
- Principle of Quality vs. Productivity (119)
- Principle of Cutting Problems in Half (122)
- The Don't Sink the Ship Principle (123)
- On Time Delivery: The Spike Principle (124)
- Principle of Pace (126)
- The Joseph Principle (127)
- Principle of "Sweating the Small Stuff" (128)
- Principle of Knowing When You're in Trouble (129)
- Principle of "Say it Once, Say it Twice..." (132)
- Sales Principle: The 30 Second Elevator Summary (133)
- The Moose Dance Principle (134)
- The "Dance with the One You Brought to the Dance" Principle (135)
- Principle of Contracting Up Front (136)
- Financial Principle of Collections (137)
- Wiggle Room Principle (140)
- Trial Basis Principle (141)
- Principle of Labor as a Fixed Asset (142)
- Decision Making: The Principle of Peace (143)

Chapter 12 .... When It's All Said and Done 145

Recommended Reading & Resources 149

Author's Biography 151

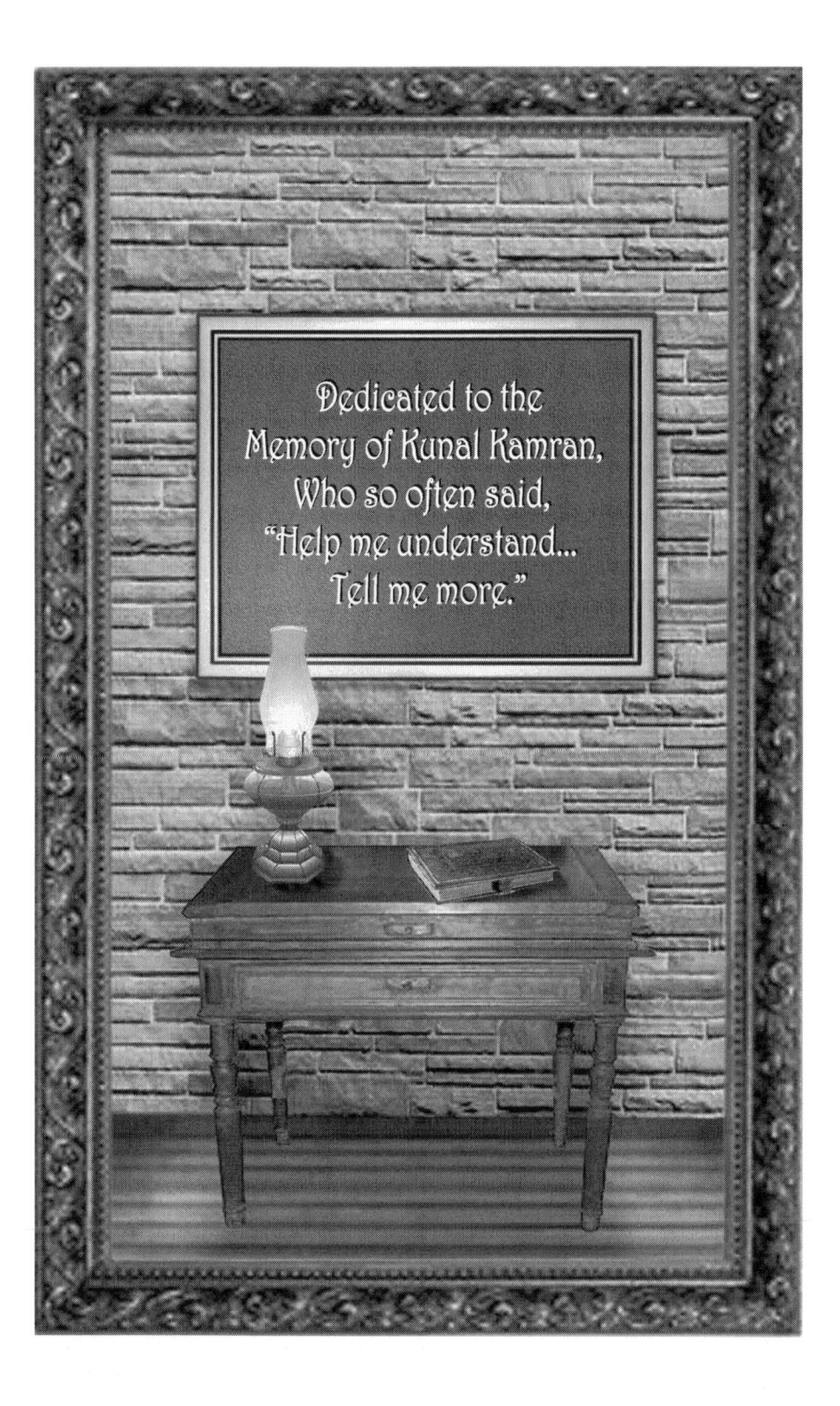

Dedicated to the
Memory of Kunal Kamran,
Who so often said,
"Help me understand...
Tell me more."

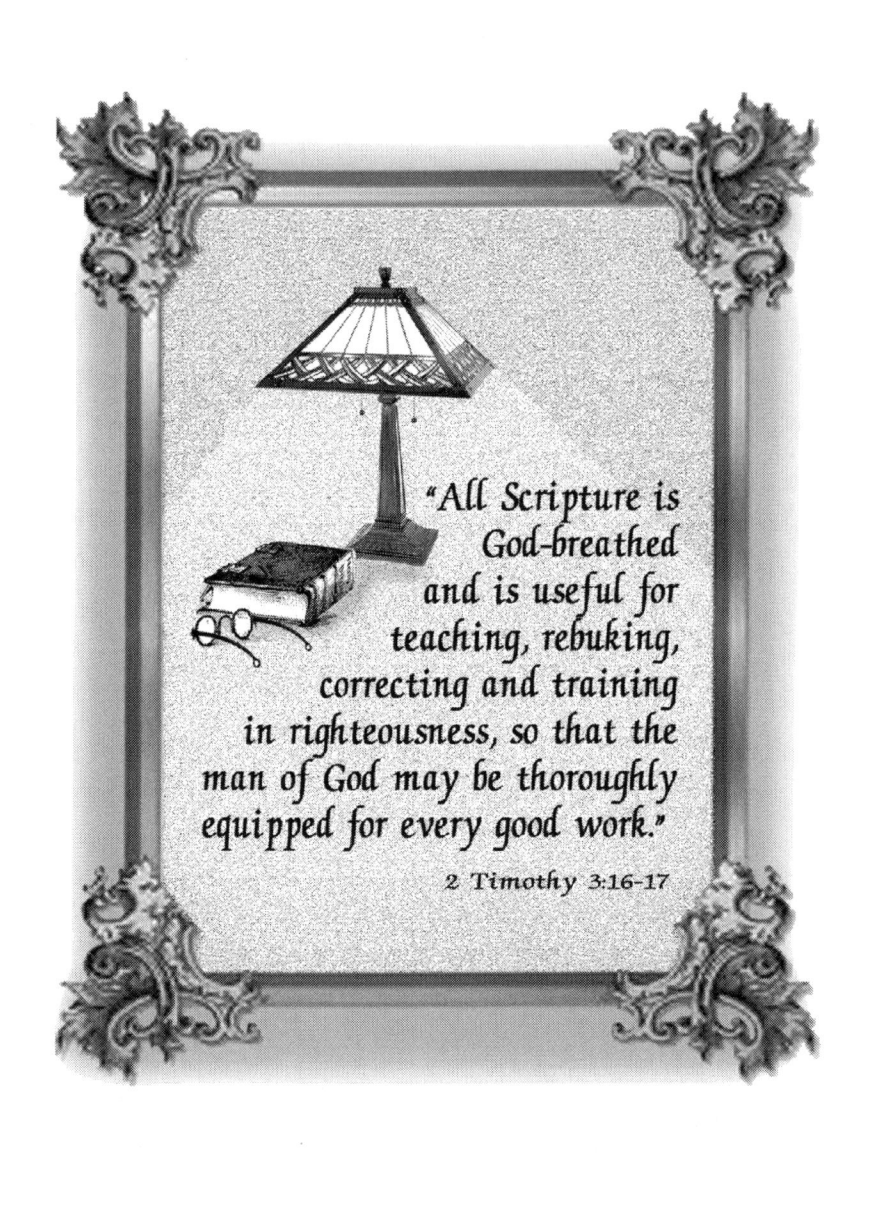

"All Scripture is God-breathed and is useful for teaching, rebuking, correcting and training in righteousness, so that the man of God may be thoroughly equipped for every good work."

2 Timothy 3:16-17

Prologue

To my children and grandchildren,

You wonder why anyone writes a book. For me, it was to share my experiences - those things that I'm passionate about, those things that have value - with you, the ones I love most.

Years ago I learned that *how* you achieve success far outweighs *what* you actually accomplish. Long after the memories of a company's achievements have dimmed, the people you worked with will still recall the way you treated them.

In **Legacy**, I share the principles and values that have guided my life. But penning the practical application of principles and values is no easy thing to do. That's because there is an essential combination of *methodology* and *heart attitude* woven together in the practice of "principled management" - a combination that is difficult to express in words. In fact, I believe that if the best of writers could pen some kind of "formula" for management success, there still would be no guarantee that it would work. Why? Because, to be successful in the practice of management, you need to have the right values and principles *combined with* the right heart attitude. Hopefully, sharing these experiences will be helpful to others. But if so, it will only be because of what those managers already possess in their personal character and beliefs. Principles do not help the unprincipled. And formulas for success, without the proper heart attitude, are generally manipulative at best.

So that's why I decided to write this book for you and for your children and grandchildren. I enjoy sharing stories about principles, and if my recollections have any influence on you and your families, I would consider that a most worthy "legacy."

Think about the stories I've already shared with you over the years - stories of your great-grandpa Duncanson, for example. They're not just entertaining – they're inspiring.

Remember the account of your great-grandpa returning from World War I and being offered a military career by his commanding officer? Remember his response? He replied, *"Well, first of all, I have some hunting I'd like to do and you know, I hear they're getting good money for beaver pelts, so after hunting I think I'll take up trapping. And after that I think I'd like to do some fishing. And then it'll be time for hunting again."* I shared that story with you because it struck me early on in life that Great-Grandpa had made a decision concerning what he valued in life and how he wanted to live life - and that's exactly what he did. I could wish nothing more for you.

And that brings up a question: How will you take measure of your life?

I believe that *serving others* must at least be part of your assessment. In Matthew 25, verses 31-40, we read:

*"When the Son of Man comes in his glory, and all the angels with him, he will sit on his glorious throne. All the nations will be gathered before him, and he will separate the people one from another as a shepherd separates the sheep from the goats. He will put the sheep on his right and the goats on his left. Then the King will say to those on his right, 'Come, you who are blessed by my Father; take your inheritance, the kingdom prepared for you since the creation of the world. For I was hungry and you gave me something to eat, I was thirsty and you gave me something to drink, I was a stranger and you invited me in, I needed clothes and you clothed me, I was sick and you looked after me, I was in prison and you came to visit me.' Then the righteous will answer him, 'Lord, when did we see you hungry and feed you, or thirsty and give you something to drink? When did we see you a stranger and invite you in, or needing clothes and clothe you? When did we see you sick or in prison and go to visit you?' The King will reply, 'Truly I tell you, **whatever you did for one of the least of these brothers and sisters of mine, you did for me.**'"*

Connect this scripture with what the Lord has to say in John 13:34 when he tells us to *"love one another"* and the way to assess your life becomes clearer. I don't want to mislead you into a works-only oriented life, however, so let me clearly state what I believe:

I believe I was created for God's glory.

"Bring my sons from afar and my daughters from the ends of the earth - everyone who is called by my name, whom I created for my glory, whom I formed and made." Isaiah 43:6-7

I believe that my life, therefore, is to be lived to serve His purposes.

"So whether you eat or drink or whatever you do, do it all for the glory of God." 1 Corinthians 10:31

I believe that my relationship with Jesus as my Savior and Lord makes living for God's glory possible and, conversely, that without that relationship, such a life is impossible.

"Whoever believes in him (Jesus) is not condemned, but whoever does not believe stands condemned already because they have not believed in the name of God's one and only Son." John 3:18

"I have been crucified with Christ and I no longer live, but Christ lives in me. The life I now live in the body, I live by faith in the Son of God, who loved me and gave himself for me." Galatians 2:20

"I can do all things through Christ who strengthens me." Philippians 4:13

"And this is his command: to believe in the name of his Son, Jesus Christ, and to love one another as he commanded us. The one who keeps God's commands lives in him, and he in them." I John 5:23-24a

I believe that the Holy Spirit gives me understanding, desire and guidance to do those things the Lord would have me do.

"And this is how we know that he lives in us: We know it by the Spirit he gave us." I John 5:24b

"What we have received is not the spirit of the world, but the Spirit who is from God, so that we may understand what God has freely given us." 1 Corinthians 2:12

When a person first comes to believe that Jesus is the Son of God and that He died for our sins, it's often a big event in one's life. Growing in a personal relationship with the Lord and maturing spiritually, however, usually takes many years. Similarly, I didn't come to my philosophy of management all at once. It took years of experience and lots of successes and failures before I reached a level of understanding of my life's purpose (and I attribute that understanding to the Lord). But eventually I came to where I could state with conviction that my personal mission in life was to be a "steward" of what was given me to manage and that my mission was to carry out my role as a "servant leader," using the skills that the Lord gave me and giving God the credit for whatever was accomplished.

This realization and definitive personal life mission meant everything to me. Why? Because *I knew I was where I was supposed to be in life.* I knew that what I was doing was in line with what the Lord wanted me to do.

Did this mean I lead the "perfect life"? Not by any means. I fought all the temptations common to man and I got tired and frustrated with how things were going from time to time. But in general, I experienced a peace and a joy that continually confirmed my role in life.

With this confirmation I can tell you that in most management situations I felt confident of what we were doing. There were times, however, when the Lord led me into situations where I was out of my comfort zone - for His purposes and my growth. Let me share one such story:

The management team had implemented our strategic plan and the company's performance was consistently outstanding. I was feeling very comfortable in my leadership role at work. That's when I was "reminded" that I was to be a servant in my personal life as well.

One evening while driving home, the Lord prompted me to paint my neighbor's house. Byron had died on Good Friday after years of struggling with Parkinson's Disease, leaving his loving wife, Dolly, a widow. I don't know why I hadn't noticed it before, but the house was very much in need of paint.

How did the Lord prompt me? All I can tell you is that I had become more sensitive to the Spirit's leading and had learned the importance of heeding those promptings. This was clearly the Lord letting me know that He wanted me to paint Dolly's house.

You already know, of course, that I am a terrible painter. I get more paint on myself than on the project. Actually, I really *hate* painting. But I was not about to ignore the Lord's leading, so I called a painter I knew and asked if he could paint Dolly's house. My thought was to simply pay him to have the job done. But he turned me down flat, saying he was swamped with work and couldn't possibly take on another job. And I got the same story from other painters I contacted. It was clear. The Lord wanted *me* to paint Dolly's house - not just to job it out to someone else.

About that time, Dolly called me (I had not yet spoken to her about this) and in the course of the conversation, she mentioned that Byron had been planning to paint their 140 year old cedar farm house but never got to it. That was all I needed. I shared with Dolly that the Lord had led me to paint her house and asked if she would be ok with that. Dolly was thrilled! And, being a Christian, she understood the Lord's working in things like this.

The rest is history. Mom and I, with help from three friends (one who had a spray gun), scraped, taped, puttied and painted Dolly's home.

So why would the Lord urge me to do something I was not skilled at doing – something I actually hated doing? Well, I've learned that the Lord does that at times to teach us that there is nothing we can't do with His help and that we shouldn't always stick to those things within our comfort zone. This experience also helped keep me humble and reminded me to give God the credit (the praise) for the good things that happen in life.

Legacy takes you through management topics and experiences that demonstrate the absolute need for having a **foundation** built on values. Your values, your beliefs and what you hold to be your personal mission in life affect everything you do. In sharing these management topics with you, I pray that you will see evidence of this in each chapter and that you will pass these values on from generation to generation - for that indeed would be a true legacy.

> *Let love and faithfulness never leave you; bind them around your neck, write them on the tablet of your heart. Then you will win favor and a good name in the sight of God and man. Trust in the LORD with all your heart and lean not on your own understanding; in all your ways acknowledge him, and he will make your paths straight. Do not be wise in your own eyes; fear the LORD and shun evil. This will bring health to your body and nourishment to your bones.*
>
> Proverbs 3:3-8

Chapter 1
What You Should Know About Yourself

- Your Personal Values and Life Purpose
- Your Personal Assessment
  - ✓ Your Strengths – How You Can Help Others
  - ✓ Your Weaknesses – How Others Can Help You
  - ✓ Your Change Plan – The Wheel of Life
  - ✓ Keeping Yourself Grounded – Keeping in Balance
- Your Personal Discipline

Chapter One is about building a strong personal foundation for your life. To be effective as a servant leader, you must first be solidly grounded in your values and life purpose. You need to know your strengths and weaknesses and especially need to be honest about your weaknesses, filling those gaps by relying on the strengths of others. This takes personal discipline and something else that most managers fail to embrace – listening to the honest opinions of others. Be sure to take your time as you read this section of Legacy.

Love,

Dad

Your Personal Values and Life Purpose

When you graduated from high school, wouldn't it have been nice to have known what your purpose in life would be? You could have made all kinds of decisions at that time to prepare for your career, your marriage, where you were going to live and so on. No mistakes. No diversions. Just plow on toward your purpose in life.

But life is not that easy. When we were younger, we tended to respond more to our immediate circumstances, making decisions as best we could and while we may have had some longer term goals, we seldom knew where they would lead us.

There are all sorts of events outside our control that force us to make decisions we never thought we'd have to make. That's the nature of growing up. That's the nature of life. Fortunately, as we grow older, there are generally "stages" when our life purpose emerges and, over time, when that life purpose becomes clearer.

In my case it started with falling in love with Mom, although it took me awhile to get there. Here's my story:

I was born and raised in Mondovi, a rural Wisconsin farming community where everyone knew everyone. Looking back, it was the ideal place to grow up. I was blessed with four grandparents and two great-grandparents who lived nearby. On Sunday afternoons, my best friend, Chuck, and I would hop on our bicycles and visit our grandparents. We were always greeted with homemade cookies and milk.

I cherished my relationship with my grandparents and especially with my Grandpa Duncanson. I remember tagging along with him as we walked around his farm listening to one of his many stories. Along the way, Grandpa would stop by an apple tree and share how he had grafted in branches from other apple trees to produce several varieties on one tree. He would tell me about his black walnut trees which he continued to plant into his eighties. He would show me where he transplanted wild asparagus and explain why this produced a heartier crop. I listened in awe to his tales of hunting and fishing. I loved staying overnight at Grandma and Grandpa Duncanson's house, sleeping under their Hudson Bay wool blankets in the upstairs bedroom. I can still recall the smells of the room - the sounds outside - I remember it all.

A child's values are formed early in life, influenced by how your parents raised you, how they recognized your accomplishments and redirected you when you got out of line. The lessons you learned in church and in school, the code of conduct learned in organizations such as the Boy Scouts - all of these experiences instill values in a child. I was fortunate to have all of these influences in my upbringing — especially by my Grandpa Duncanson. His outlook on life seemed so simple and understandable, his understanding of nature was profound, and his respect for and kindness toward others was impressed upon me. I saw the respect that others rendered him and was proud to be his grandson. Over the years, my personal values became closely aligned with those of my grandfather.

My family lived across the street from a small lake where I fished, summer and winter. My brother Bob and I swam and canoed on that lake and ice skated in the winter. We also spent time on our grandparents' farms, helping with chores like haying in the summer months. In the fall, we hunted pheasants and, as was our family tradition, we hunted deer during Thanksgiving.

When I was eight I got my own dog. Rusty was a young golden retriever and it didn't take long for us to bond. Wanting to do things right, I went to the library and checked out a book on training dogs. I trained and raised Rusty. I fed him. I groomed him. I even dressed up like a frontiersman and marched in the local parades with Rusty prancing in front of me. I took Rusty swimming and exploring. And when my dad and brother hunted pheasants, I was always in the middle of the line because Rusty obeyed my commands. Where I went Rusty went. He was my dog.

I always thought that Mondovi was a wonderful place to grow up and never thought about not living there, but when my father was offered a promotion in the postal service, we moved to Rapid City,

South Dakota. Starting my junior year in high school, the most traumatic event for me that year was giving up Rusty (dogs weren't allowed where we were moving). As I mentioned earlier, events outside of our control often force us to make decisions we hadn't planned to make. I gave Rusty to my friend, Mike who lived on a farm where Rusty could run and run – but as I pulled out of the driveway I could see that Rusty didn't understand my leaving him. I cried all the way home.

In less than a year, another promotion for my dad took us to South St. Paul, Minnesota where I enrolled in a large high school, but not before attending a National Science Foundation summer program in mathematics at the University of Illinois. Attending three high schools and summer college in three years gave me a unique perspective on different groups of people and their values. The main "constant" for me was academics and sports. I was good in both. And while I received a West Point nomination upon graduation, at that time it was not something I saw as being my purpose in life. I declined the scholarship (note: the Viet Nam War was going on at the time and my plans at 18 years old didn't include nine years of military service and possible involvement in a war). Instead, I enrolled at the University of Minnesota where I met your mom.

It's funny now that I think about it. Sure, I had plans. In fact, I was pretty sure I was going to be a dentist — believe it or not. But there was nothing in me that I would have called a "burning desire" until I enrolled in a speech class where I met your mother. From that point on, I experienced my first clear purpose since graduation and nothing else seemed to matter. I was convinced that this was the girl I was going to marry. Our first date was in May 1969. We married in January 1970.

It's worth noting that the Viet Nam War was a significant example of an event outside of my control that forced me to make a decision I hadn't planned to make. Congress had enacted a draft, determined by lottery, to supply the men needed for war. My lottery number was 40 and since I did not have enough credits to sustain a student deferment, I knew that I would soon be drafted. My options, none of which thrilled me, were limited to:

- Wait to be drafted into the Army as a foot soldier - a two year commitment and almost assuredly receive overseas combat orders.
- Voluntarily enlist in the active Army for four years - with a ground forces combat assignment also a certainty.
- Enlist in the National Guards or Reserves for six years - with a higher likelihood of staying home after four months of active duty.
- Move to Canada.
- Go to prison.

It was the spring of 1971 and we were expecting our first child. While the military was not part of my purpose in life, raising a family with your mom was. I chose to enlist in the National Guards on a Tuesday and was sworn in that night and scheduled for basic training that summer. I had cut it close, for that Friday I received my draft notice.

Ironically, while only three years earlier I declined a West Point nomination, after completing my basic and advanced training I then enrolled in Officers Candidate School. My thought at that time was that if I was going to be in the National Guards for six years I might as well make the most of it. In fact, I actually extended my commitment and served for ten years, making a valued contribution to the military as a training coordinator, helping fellow soldiers achieve certifications that readied them for promotions. For the most part, I enjoyed my time in the service even though I never considered myself a military type.

In the early years of our marriage, one of the decisions Mom and I made was where we wanted to live and raise our family. We had experienced the hubbub of the city and its growing crime and after a few years agreed that this was not where we wanted to raise our children. But Mom had made another decision I didn't know about. She had accepted Jesus as her Savior and, in her love for me, quietly prayed that I would come to know the Lord.

One weekend we traveled to Lake Pepin. There was a plot of land for sale we wanted to see so we packed a picnic lunch and made the drive along the Mississippi River. It was a beautiful fall day and I can still remember lying in the field with your mom, dreaming about what it would be like to live there. The scenery was beautiful and the price was reasonable. How could we go wrong?

Your mom, while supportive of purchasing the land, had already adopted the practice of praying about major decisions before making them. By this time I was aware that Mom had become more "religious" - and I was trying to be respectful of that change - but this was a "no-brainer" decision in my mind. We should buy the land before someone else did. Nevertheless, I told her that I would "pray" about the purchase (a foolish thing for an insincere person to do). I asked God to "give me a sign" if He *didn't* want us to buy the land (an even more foolish request).

Although I was totally convinced that we were about to make the transaction, the very next day your Mom brought me a copy of the Star Tribune featuring a front page article about a freak storm on Lake Pepin. The local sheriff, a distant cousin of mine, was quoted as saying, *"I've never seen anything like it. There were ten foot waves on the lake."* As I read the story, I realized that this was not a mere coincidence. When I shared what had happened with an elderly Christian man I knew, he pointed his finger at me and said, *"God is working on you."* We decided not to go ahead with the purchase.

Our decision proved timely, because shortly thereafter I was out of work for thirteen weeks. The Lord had other plans for us. And so did your mother.

Without my knowledge, your mom had enrolled me in a Bill Gothard Institute in Basic Life Principles conference. Since I had no job, I was now free to attend all five evening sessions. During the last session I clearly heard the gospel message and asked the Lord to take over my life. It's hard to describe, but it was like a weight was lifted from my twenty-five year old shoulders and I looked at everything differently. In addition to looking for work during those thirteen weeks of unemployment, I read the Bible. I had read Scripture before, but now for the first time, I *understood* what Jesus had done for me.

One of the most touching memories of that time was when an elderly woman came to our apartment. Though she had few possessions, she had learned that I was out of work and brought from her pantry whatever groceries she could spare. It was like the story of the widow's pennies. As we looked through what she had given us, I still remember coming across a can of garbanzo beans. I didn't know what they were, but now, every time I see garbanzo beans I think of that lady's kindness.

For most, looking for work can be disheartening, but not for me. I determined that the Lord was handling everything and therefore I was going to be positive and open to whatever came my way. I got up every morning, put on my suit and tie, and went to the library to pour over copies of Standard & Poors and Moody's business directories. I searched for companies that I felt would be good ones to work for and I mailed application after application. I went on job interviews lined up by a recruiter with whom I was working but despite many interviews, there was only one offer – and that came from Canada Life Insurance.

I had spent several hours at Canada Life completing profile tests and being interviewed. Interestingly, one of the interviewers gave me a copy of <u>Good News for Modern Man</u>. One may have thought that was a sign that I should accept their offer of employment but by now I had adopted your mom's practice of praying before making decisions - and I did not feel that this was where the Lord wanted me to be. I declined the offer from Canada Life Insurance.

A few days later I received a call from the owner of a manufacturing firm in St. Paul. He introduced himself and said, *"I hear* you're looking for work and I'm looking for an office manager." He asked me to come to his office and meet with him right away. In the interview I learned that he had gotten my resume from the manager at Canada Life, following a conversation they had on the elevator. I was offered the position, went home and talked to your mom and prayed about this job. I was convinced that this is where the Lord wanted me. How else could you explain being offered a job for which you hadn't applied? I started the following week.

Working in manufacturing was a wonderful experience. I learned about systems, controls and processes that made an operation run smoothly. I also learned about people management, basic marketing concepts and customer service. A year after I started I was promoted to Assistant General Manager and shortly thereafter I became the General Manager of the company. Mom and I resumed our search to move from the city.

We looked within a 50 mile commuting distance and after searching the nearby rural communities chose to rent an old restored farmhouse on a private estate near Osceola, Wisconsin. It was only an hour's drive to St. Paul and an hour and a half from where I grew up. While it may not have been fully evident to us at the time, what we were really doing was making a decision about our life purpose. Moving to the country to raise our family was a significant step in that direction.

Two years later I took a management position in Osceola at another manufacturing firm. I worked there for ten years. No more commuting to the city. More time with the family. Less pay, but that, too, was a values decision. Where and how we would live carried more importance than how much income we would have.

It's interesting that once you begin making decisions based on your personal values and life purpose, one thing builds on another. For example, our joint decision that Mom would stay home with you children seemed right - as did the decision to home-school you for much of your education. These could have been considered "sacrifices" but they were really values decisions. Mom had her life purpose before her. It was working with children – our own and eventually others. My life purpose became evident over time. I enjoyed helping others become the best they could be. I chose to serve others as a manager and a steward of the business.

In Covey's The Seven Habits of Highly Effective People I learned to "begin with the end in mind." Stephen Covey stressed the importance of aligning myself with what he called "true north" principles, mentioning "character" and "ethics" and asking me to consider how, at the end of my life, I would want others to speak of me. Covey's "habits" and the concept of having a personal life mission are timeless truths. I saw how the Lord's values, expressed in scripture, and a life purpose to "be in His will" were my best path.

We made plenty of mistakes in life, but Mom and I never regretted those decisions that were grounded in our personal values and our life's purpose. Nor, I believe, will you.

As you read Legacy, consider what your life purpose is. Here's a good exercise to help you with this:

- First "look out" to the end of your life.
    - ✓ Where are you?
    - ✓ What have you accomplished?
- Now "turn around and look back."
    - ✓ Try to see all the things you have done to get where you are.
    - ✓ How do you feel about where you are?
    - ✓ What do you want to be able to say about your life?
    - ✓ What would you like others to say about you?
- Now consider what has real lasting value and think about your life purpose.
- Write down your personal mission statement and review it regularly until you are comfortable with what you have determined is important as your life's purpose.

Your Personal Assessment

The military has one of the best training programs I've ever experienced. As early as the mid-seventies the Army had audio-visual programs for nearly every required military skill component. Considering that VHS didn't come on the market until the late seventies, the military's approach was far ahead of its time.

My role in running the military training room was to assess each individual soldier for the required competencies. Their supervisors would then test their field skills during active duty training. These tests were compared to the military's qualification requirements, the gaps were identified and I would then schedule training in those areas to bring the soldiers' competencies to a level that would qualify them for promotion.

This was a simple and effective training system. The military's expected outcome was troop readiness. The individual soldier's reward was promotion and an increased pay level. It worked.

But it all starts with a personal assessment.

How do you assess yourself? There are many tools for doing this and I recommend you use several. Profiles that compare the likes and dislikes of others to those of your own can help you see potential careers (based on the theory that you're likely to be more successful and happier doing those things you enjoy). The Strong Interest Inventory® and the Achiever® are examples of such profiles. I generally use these in conjunction with the Myers-Briggs Type Indicator® as career counseling tools. They are available as on-line tests and should be reviewed with a trained counselor.

Over the years I have been surprised at how many talented young people I've met who have never taken a career assessment profile. I've been equally impressed with how surprised they are following an assessment. A typical response is *"That's me! How did this test know that?"*

Knowing yourself, your likely behaviors, your strengths and your weaknesses is critical to job enjoyment and relationship development. In fact, I think it's probably just as important to know what you're *not* good at as it is to know what you are good at. More on that later.

Your Strengths – How You Can Help Others

Most people have a fair idea of their strengths. They've experienced success enough times, heard compliments from others and realize what their skills are.

I believe that the skills you possess are a gift from God. In Matthew 25, Jesus shares the story of a man who trusted three of his servants with "talents" (money of differing amounts) as he went on a trip. When he returned, he learned that two of his servants used their God-given skills to gain a good return, for which they were commended. The third, however, for fear of failing, did nothing and simply returned the money he was to have invested. His master was not at all pleased with this.

The teaching is clear: the Lord gives each of us talents (in terms of our *skills* - not necessarily money) and we are responsible for putting those skills to good use. The Bible teaches what Jesus will consider important when believers come face to face with Him in the resurrection. Be sure to read further in Matthew 25 about the deeds of kindness that were done to others. The Lord expects His followers to use the gifts He has given them to love one another and he will judge us accordingly.

> "I the Lord search the heart and examine the mind, to reward each person according to their conduct, according to what their deeds deserve." Jeremiah 17:10

Throughout the Bible our Lord instructs us to love one another, serve one another and encourage one another and in so doing, His will is carried out by His people on earth: *"Whatever you did for one of the least of these brothers of mine, you did for me."*

Generally, people gravitate to careers that play to their strengths. Like the pro golfer's comment, *"I get paid for doing what I really enjoy – golf,"* choosing a career where you can play to your strengths is ideal. Combining your ideal career with your personal life mission can result in a most rewarding vocation. If possible, this is what you should strive for. Unfortunately, people too often work in careers where they lack the passion for their jobs. These folks often take on an avocation where they can exercise their strengths and experience the enjoyment they're seeking - and there's nothing wrong with that.

In either case, once you've determined what your real strengths are - those gifts you've been given - I challenge you to use your talents to help others. Become known as the person to come to when someone needs your particular skill. Become known for being available to help others.

Your Weaknesses – How Others Can Help You

Typically, when a person is strong in one area, there is a corresponding weakness in another part of his life. For example, highly empathetic people often lack the ability to see the realistic hard facts, whereas detailed-oriented "nuts & bolts" people sometimes lack the ability to "feel in" on things. Using profile tools can help you understand your weaknesses. Seeking honest feedback from co-workers and loved ones, while difficult, is also a valuable way to learn about yourself. The Scottish poet, Robert Burns, wrote:

"O would some power the gift to give us to see ourselves as others see us."

Proverbs 16:13 teaches the value of receiving this feedback:

"Kings take pleasure in honest lips; they value the one who speaks what is right."

When selecting members of a management team, I considered it just as important to recognize the weaknesses in each manager as to know their strengths. As the management team began to develop an interdependency of trust, I encouraged them to pair off with the person who could best shore them up in those areas where they were not strong - someone who would give honest feedback. As examples, the "get-it-done" guy paired up with the "details-oriented" manager. The "output" guy sought help from the "people" person. And over time, the team eventually experienced an appreciation for and recognition of each other's strengths, coupled with a healthy self-deprecating attitude about their own weaknesses. I considered it a milestone when I saw the management team openly acknowledging strengths and weaknesses with each other.

In marriage the same principle applies. Spouses should seek honest feedback concerning the areas of their lives where they are not strong and together form an agreement on how things will be handled. For example, the husband who has a difficult time staying on budget should not only acknowledge this to his wife - he should also accept her role as the financial disciplinarian in the family and let her know how much he appreciates her for this. In our marriage your mom always knew when to get me back on track when I needed redirection.

Your Change Plan – The Wheel of Life

While knowing your weaknesses is important, it is not enough. Once you've identified the areas where you are lacking, you should then create a personal improvement "change plan" for these areas.

There's a simple, effective tool for determining where you need to change. It's called the **Wheel of Life** and you simply plot where *you would like to be* in each assessment area and compare that to *where you are*. The Wheel of Life is often used as a tool for coaching managers and its value is in the individual's definition of what is important to him (personal values) and his admission of where he is at.

Simply draw a wheel with five concentric circles numbered 1 through 5. Divide the wheel into as many sections as you wish to have "assessment areas." In this example, there are eight areas to be assessed.

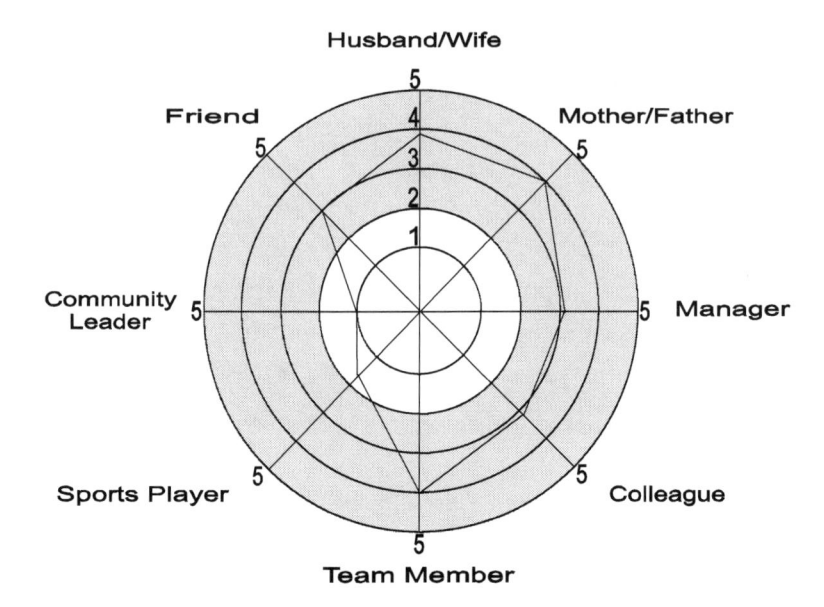

Legacy - Principled Management   About Yourself - 14

What assessment areas should you choose? Well, that's up to you, but consider what is most important to you, then the next most important thing, etc. A typical list of assessment areas would look like this:

- My spiritual relationship with the Lord
- My marriage relationship with my spouse
- My family relationship with my children, parents, grandchildren
- My career
- My health
- Financial security

Once you've created your list, then for each area on a scale of 1-5 (with 5 representing that you've met your own personal expectation of where you'd like to be on the wheel), place a dot where you believe you are today. Once you've done this with each area, then connect the dots on your wheel. This picture represents the "balance" in your life and reveals the areas where you are out of balance.

If your wheel is uneven, you're probably experiencing a bumpy ride in your life. If your wheel is concentric but small in diameter, you are probably not experiencing life in its fullest. Your desire should be to have a large round wheel, indicating that you are living as you want to be living – life in the fullest.

Your next step is to decide what you will do to close the gaps between where you want to be and where you are.

We continually change throughout our lives and need to work toward progress in those areas where our lives are out of balance. 1 Timothy 4:15 instructs us: *"Be diligent in these matters; give yourself wholly to them, so that everyone may see your progress."* By charting your own Wheel of Life, you'll be able to see your personal progress in those areas that are important to you. Share your wheel with the person you highly trust and ask for honest feedback about your improvement.

(Note: for more information, go to www.mindtools.com. The Wheel of Life graphic used by permission.)

Keeping Yourself Grounded
Keeping in Balance

In business and in marriage it's all too easy to look at your accomplishments and think more highly of yourself than you ought. While it may be true that your personal efforts have resulted in success, it is unhealthy to allow yourself to become conceited. Others in your organization and your life have undoubtedly contributed to your accomplishments and the healthy manager recognizes these people and shows appreciation for their support.

The manager who takes all the credit for his accomplishments (or the husband who sees himself as the primary contributor to the marriage) is in for a rude awakening. Those around you will easily sense an attitude of self-importance and will think less of you for it.

As we've just seen, it's important to keep yourself in balance as a manager. Refer back to your **Wheel of Life**. If you're devoting too much time to your work and neglecting your health or your family, you will not only pay a hefty price for being out of balance, others will lose respect for you. One way to avoid getting out of balance is to be a part of an "accountability group" – people you trust and meet with regularly for the purpose of sharing successes and failures, ideas and concerns. This is done in a setting of strict confidence, typically with business people who have similar responsibilities and values. An excellent example of an organization that offers this is CBMC's Business Forums. (www.cbmcforums.com)

What values have you grounded yourself in? Are you grounded? How do you really know? One way to reveal how grounded you are is to see how you act under pressure in a crisis. Values aren't circumstantial - they are the same in good times and bad. Can you do what is right even if it's at a personal cost? Do you avoid dishonest gain even if no one will know? This was apparently of great concern to the Apostle Paul:

> "So I strive always to keep my conscience clear before God and man." Acts 24:16

Jesus compared a believer's life to building a house and warned us to be careful about the kind of foundation we lay for the structures of that life. He told us to be sure that our foundation is firmly laid on solid "rock" so that when the storms of life come, we won't be swept away. The "rock" he was talking about was *himself*, as the Apostle Paul made very clear in 1 Corinthians 3:11:

> "...no one can lay any foundation other than the one already laid, which is Jesus Christ."

And it is our *faith* in the person and work of Jesus Christ that gives us the right to build upon the foundation he has already laid. But we must be careful how we build on that foundation for Paul also went on to say,

> "If anyone builds on this foundation using gold, silver, costly stones, wood, hay or straw, their work will be shown for what it is, because the Day will bring it to light, it will be revealed with fire, and the fire will test the quality of each person's work." 1 Corinthians 3:12-13

Remember,

> "...where your treasure is, there your heart will be also." Matthew 6:21

Your Personal Discipline

Surely you know that many runners take part in a race, but only one of them wins the prize. Run, then, in such a way as to win the prize. Every athlete in training submits to strict discipline, in order to be crowned with a wreath that will not last; but we do it for one that will last forever. That is why I run straight for the finish line; that is why I am like a boxer who does not waste his punches. I harden my body with blows and bring it under complete control, to keep myself from being disqualified after having called others to the contest.

1 Corinthians 9:24-27 (Good News Translation)

Healthy habits are pretty easy to start but often hard to sustain. Personal improvement requires personal discipline. And personal discipline is all about measurement, recognition, reward and redirection. Eating right, daily exercise, reading, sleeping well, etc., are all examples of areas where personal discipline is needed. We'll cover management techniques in the next two chapters but for now, realize that how well you perform will be a factor of your personal discipline in life.

Much of what I share in *Legacy* is about systems. Systems help us sustain repeatable, reliable processes. In a sense they help us with being "disciplined." Let me share three simple examples of personal disciplines, supported by simple systems:

I could never afford to be late to work, but when I was holding down a full time job while going to college, it would have been all too easy to hit the snooze button and oversleep. My system: I set three alarms, 2-3 minutes apart. Two were near the bed and one was in the adjacent room. And I put battery back-ups in the alarms just in case there was a power failure.

Misplaced keys are always a hassle. Did I put them on the dresser, or the counter top, or on the coffee table? It's a pretty sure bet that where I thought they were is not where they ended up. A simple system was to create a key hook where I always put the keys when not in use. The personal discipline to hang them on the hook is easy to follow.

Forgetting someone's birthday is embarrassing, but with today's contact software on our laptops and cell phones, it need never happen. The simple system I use is to enter in important dates and "to do's" with the appropriate recurrence and an alarm that gives me enough notice to buy a gift, send a card or make a call. The personal discipline required is to simply enter the information into the program with an automatic weekly back up just in case my computer crashes. This simple system takes nothing away from me creatively recognizing someone's birthday – it just relieves me of the need to remember when it is. Note: you'll see how important this system is as we explore Customer Relationship Management systems (CRM).

Chapter 2

Management Philosophy: What is Principled Management?

I still remember the spring Wisconsin opener when my grandpa took me fishing for brook trout. We got up at 4 AM and stopped by an old farmhouse to pick up a friend who was going to join us. I didn't realize until I met him that Grandpa's friend was blind. It was still dark when we arrived at the spot Grandpa had scouted out weeks earlier. With barely enough light for me to cast my line, I wondered about our blind companion. "How is he going to fish, Grandpa?" I have never forgotten his reply: "A man doesn't have to see to fish." Over many years of trout fishing his blind friend had acquired a sense of touch and feel, and a keen intuition. He simply knew, without seeing, how to catch a fish. That experience had a profound effect on me and became one of my principles: "A man doesn't have to see to fish." Just think of the many applications of that philosophy.

Chapter 2 sets the stage for the next several chapters. We will explore the foundational building blocks necessary to every business and the principles behind a number of highly effective management processes. You will learn the importance of seeing business through the viewpoint of what I call "critical business systems" and how, over time, you can develop a "sense" of when things are running smoothly.

We start by defining your management philosophy. In this chapter, you will learn about servant leadership - a management philosophy whose principles are founded in Scripture - principles that managers can integrate into their companies' values and processes. Servant leadership is not a management style. Rather, it is a personal belief structure that follows Jesus' example to be a servant to others. You will see how this applies to both your work and your family life in everything you do.

Just like Grandpa's blind friend who didn't need to see to fish, the repeated practice of the following management principles will become so engrained in who you are and what you do that you will develop a truly unique and instinctive sense of your role as a servant leader.

Love,
Dad

When I use the term, **Principled Management**, what do I mean?

My work experience revealed to me that there are a number of **systemic business processes** that are common to all businesses. As I studied the Bible, I discovered a number of scriptural principles which directly applied to these business processes and, when integrated with the company's values, produced lasting results. These timeless principles have a **servant-leadership focus** and promote the philosophy of being a **steward**.

Legacy connects the principles found in scriptures with the **systemic business processes** that are necessary in business. Making this "connection" gives purpose and meaning to managers. There's a reason why certain business processes work so well. It's because their foundation is in these principles – principles that have been there for ages, but perhaps not recognized, and certainly not acknowledged.

Let me share one example. I call it the "Joseph Principle," although it is actually only one of many principles taught in the story of Joseph. Despite being sold into slavery by his brothers, Joseph sustained his personal faith and discipline to keep a positive attitude. He acknowledged that the Lord had a plan for him — and he did! Finding favor with Pharaoh, at only 30 years of age, Joseph was given charge of the entire land of Egypt. Read in Genesis 41:47-57 how during seven years of abundant crops Joseph stored up *"huge quantities of grain, like the sand of the sea; it was so much that he stopped keeping records because it was beyond measure."* But following the seven years of abundance came seven years of famine, during which time, Joseph not only was able to supply the needs of Egypt, but to surrounding countries as well (*"all the world came to Egypt to buy grain from Joseph..."*).

While there are many lessons to be learned from the story of Joseph, one important principle is so evident - a principle that is so fundamental to business and family finances - a principle that should be a foundational building block to any business plan. That is the principle of managing the cycles of business. Every business has its ups and downs, its good years and bad. Seasoned managers recognize that, to weather the bad years, you set aside profits from the good years – reserves to carry you during those lean times. Having cash reserves eliminates the need to borrow. It allows business leaders to buffer these cycles *without* imposing on their workforce (e.g., reduced hours, layoffs, pay cuts).

Joseph knew full well what would happen had he not stored away a portion of the abundance. He knew that there would have been wastefulness and excesses, followed by his people starving during the lean years. He also recognized that it was *his* responsibility as a steward of the land of Egypt and as a servant-leader, to ensure that this would not happen.

This is but one example of *Principled Management* that is so relevant today. In **Legacy**, I will share several examples of *Principled Management* to employ in a number of business systems and practices. So what is *Principled Management*?

- *Principled Management* is the **practice** of these scriptural principles in business.

- *Principled Management* is the **recognition** of scripture as the source of these principles.

- *Principled Management* is the **demonstration** of a servant leadership belief structure.

- *Principled Management* is the **definition** of your business ethics.

- *Principled Management* is the **umbrella** under which all of your business decisions are made.

Principled Management's **foundational building blocks** are:

- Vision, Mission & Values
- Strategic Customer-Focused Business Plan
- Strategic Marketing & Sales Plan
- Information & Communications Systems
- Human Resources Plan
- Critical Business Systems
- Performance Management System

Implementing *Principled Management* practices in business:

- Creates purpose for the management team's performance...
- Connects employees and their jobs with serving customers...
- Educates employees to the bottom line in a meaningful way.

The result achieved from the practice of *Principled Management* is an educated management team that is:

- Focused on the company's vision and mission...
- Centered on serving customers...
- Motivated by performance.

Principled Management produces a customer-focused workforce whose performance is connected to the bottom line.

Principled Management improves company-wide communications about things that really matter.

Principled Management improves operational performance.

CHAPTER 3
VISION MISSION & VALUES

Everything starts with a vision. In every start-up the business owner had some type of <u>Vision</u> of what he saw his company becoming. Principled Management takes it further than that by declaring the <u>Values</u> you will live by - values that dictate how you will do business. Principled Management defines the <u>Mission</u> as the "road you will travel" on your journey toward your <u>Vision</u>.

This chapter is critical to business planning and cannot be skipped over. Too many business owners dream about the benefits of their business, how they will spend the profits, the perks from being in business, etc., but this is not where Principled Management starts. There is a longer term purpose for the principled manager.

Once again, see how these teachings readily apply to your personal and family life. Do you have a vision of who you want to become? Are you firmly grounded in your values? Do you know the road you'll be traveling through life?

Enjoy this chapter of *Legacy*.

Love,
Dad

VISION
"the end in mind"

As a business leader you must have a vision. Zig Ziglar says, *"If you aim at nothing, you will hit it every time!"* So you must have a vision. And, as we will see, you must also define your mission. Finally, as the owner and leader of the company, you are the one responsible for declaring the values your company will live by.

In defining "vision" we should take Covey's advice to *"begin with the end in mind."* Our time on this earth is finite and given the limited number of years you have to establish a business, the place to start is to consider what you would like to have accomplished by the end of your career. In other words, *"look out – turn around – and look back."*

Reflect on what would merit a response like that in Matthew 25:21, *"Well done, good and faithful servant!"* Your vision statement should be idealistic and broad in its scope. Here are some examples of vision statements:

"To become the leading training organization to the environmental controls industry in North America."

"To become the premier golf tour agency for Scottish golf tourists."

"To be recognized as the industrial cleaning supplies company that the market looks to for products, service and technical support in the Midwest."

"To provide caring drug/alcohol counseling services to those who cannot afford conventional rehab programs."

I also recommend that you state a further definition of "success" in your vision, such as the following example:

"How will we know that we are nearing our vision? When we see...

- an educated workforce with a good understanding of how their combined efforts impact the company's success - a workforce that is recognized and rewarded accordingly,

- a workforce whose standard of living is improving,

- a cohesive management team embracing a common set of values and looking forward to the long term growth and health of the company,

- a diversified product line that is continually improving in its features and benefits, as well as its margins,

- a loyal customer base of over (number) of clients, no one of which represents more than (%) of total revenues; customers who see value in partnering with us,

- a work environment where management and employees care for one another's well-being, and,

- a truly virtuous business cycle where the policies, practices, culture and business systems all promote continued improvement and growth."

As we move on, you will see how everything flows from your company's vision.

What is your vision? I encourage you to think deep thoughts about your company, your personal role in your job and your family. Ask yourself, "How will I know that I'm moving toward my vision? What evidences should I be able to see?"

MISSION

"the road you'll be traveling down"

The best way to think of a mission is to consider yourself on a journey, one that hopefully takes you to your vision. As with any trip you make, there are a number of roads you can take. There's the expressway, there are county roads and there are scenic rustic roads with winding turns and narrow passes. While some paths are more direct and may get you to where you're going in less time, there is often a price to pay for taking that route (let's call it a "toll way"), whereas other routes are less stressful and more enjoyable.

Whichever route you choose as you journey toward your vision, *that* becomes your mission - and the roadmap should be laid out for everyone in the organization to see.

Mission statements share the direction you are heading and the routes you plan to take (and by inference, therefore, those routes you will *not* be taking). Your mission statement should provide simple and clear direction for all employees. Here are some examples:

> "Stewart Bros. Plumbing's mission is to provide 24 hour quick response service to residents in Washington County."

> "The mission of Future Scholars is to provide every 6th grade student in Minong with a lap top computer."

"Boulder Construction's mission is to offer low cost affordable single family homes, built on site, for families who qualify under the HUD-2310 initiative."

"Thomas Engineering's mission is to serve design engineers in the aerospace industry with small run fabricated metal prototypes, design services, technical and testing support."

"Quick Serve's mission is to provide a complete oil and filter change and five point safety inspection in 20 minutes or less."

When you read a mission statement, you should be able to easily see what the company intends to do. In the examples above, Stewart Bros. is not making this offer to customers in Chisago County. Future Scholars is not offering 5th graders a computer nor are they offering computers to other communities. Boulder Construction is not building luxury homes nor are they working with those who do not qualify under the special HUD program. Thomas Engineering is focusing on small run developmental work with engineers in a specific industry. Could they serve others? Possibly, but their mission has them traveling down this path at this time.

Notice Quick Serve's mission to provide their service in 20 minutes or less. It's an easy mission to understand and speaks of all sorts of systems, policies and procedures Quick Serve will need to have to achieve this mission. This brings up the *principle of measurement*. When you read a mission statement, it should reveal what things will need to be measured to ensure that the company is on the right track. In the section on Performance Management we will cover the importance of measurement.

Mission statements should be reviewed at least annually although that does not necessarily mean that they need to change. As long as the mission defines the road you wish to travel, it is adequate, but if you decide to head down a different path, it needs to be reflected in a revised mission statement.

Just as all employees need to know the vision of the company, they also need to know the mission. Keep your mission statement simple. In employee meetings and other communications continually share the vision and mission of the company. Quiz your employees on it. Look for everyone to be able to recite the mission. Why? Because the specific objectives that you and your management team will be creating each year all flow from the mission statement, which, in turn, should be moving you toward the company's vision.

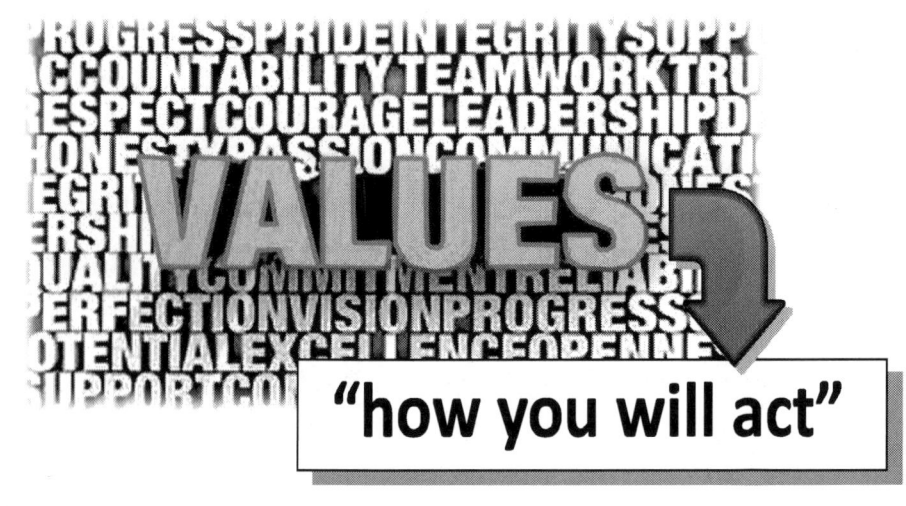

VALUES: "how you will act"

We've learned that the vision is the "end in mind" and that the mission states "the road you'll be traveling down." Your company's values, therefore, define how you will act as you travel down this road toward your vision. Think of them as guideposts to keep you on the straight and narrow. Several passages in scripture speak to this:

> *"The integrity of the upright guides them, but the unfaithful are destroyed by their duplicity."* Proverbs 12:17

> *"The Lord detests lying lips but he delights in people who are trustworthy."* Proverbs 12:22

> *"My steps have held to your paths; my feet have not stumbled."* Psalm 17:5

> *"Teach me your way, lord; lead me in a straight path..."* Psalm 27:11

> *"Your word is a lamp for my feet, a light on my path."* Psalm 119:105

"I instruct you in the way of wisdom and lead you along straight paths." Proverbs 4:11

"Whoever walks in integrity walks securely, but whoever takes crooked paths will be found out." Proverbs 10:9

"Bear with each other and forgive whatever grievances you may have against one another." Colossians 3:13

"I appeal...that all of you agree with one another in what you say and that there may be no divisions among you, but that you may be perfectly united in mind and thought." I Corinthians 1:10 – 13

State your values clearly so they can be easily understood by employees. Below are some examples of value statements:

"We respect one another and recognize the value of diversity."

"At Burroughs Printing, there is no racial or gender discrimination."

"Peterson's Meats recognizes a strong work ethic."

"We live our values and agree to confront one another when we feel that our values are being violated."

"We value the ability of each person to work responsibly without supervision."

"Douglas Ford values the combined efforts of the team."

"There is not even the slightest hint of sexual harassment condoned here."

"Pay for performance is our standard."

"Honesty is always the best policy."

"At Cumberland Clothing, we admit our mistakes, correct the practices, and move on."

"We believe in promoting the most qualified individual, from within the company, whenever possible."

Share stories that demonstrate your values. Here is one such story:

Mary was a valued member of the company's design team. Unfortunately, she was involved in a serious car accident and suffered injuries that, while not life-threatening, required that she stay home for several weeks. As a single mom, Mary could not afford the loss of income and her team members knew that. Although restricted, Mary was capable of doing some work from home and her manager approved that and made arrangements for team members to drop off and pick up her work assignments. While this part time accommodation provided Mary with some pay, she would still face a financial hardship during her recovery.

After a few days, however, the design team approached their manager with a proposal. They offered to take on the work that Mary could not do, even though that would mean extra hours for them (and since they were salaried, at no extra pay), in return for which they asked that the company keep Mary at full pay while working part time from home.

The company's values statement included "We care about one another and support one another when needed." This was an important corporate value and here was a prime example of a team reaching out to support one of its own during a time of need. The management was touched by this outreach from Mary's co-workers and wholeheartedly supported the proposal to keep her on full time pay.

This company's story should be told in every new employee orientation. Sharing the company's values is such an important task that I personally conducted that portion of orientations. The values come from the leader of the company and the introduction of values to employees is, therefore, the leader's responsibility. It's that important. In fact, business leaders should actually look for opportunities to demonstrate their companies' values. I call these opportunities "values in action."

I was fortunate to have had a number of opportunities in my career to witness "values in action." The following story shares how these experiences helped shape my values as a business leader:

As a student, I had a job at a restaurant chain starting as a busboy and working my way up to a cook and eventually, the restaurant manager. The owner, Doc, was an outstanding "people person" and possessed a natural ability to connect with employees and customers. I was fortunate to have Doc as a mentor and a friend.

Doc recognized the value of knowing people and took a sincere interest in what was going on in their lives. If he did not know a customer who entered the restaurant, he took it upon himself to meet that person and find out something about them. The next time that customer came in, Doc would greet him by name.

Doc gave of himself by spending time with employees during their breaks and learning what was going on in their lives. People were important to Doc and he would go out of his way to help them whenever he could. This was recognized by customers, who in turn were loyal in their patronage. It was recognized by suppliers, who learned that if you did what you promised, Doc would be your long term customer. And it was recognized by employees, who worked not only for the pay, but because they enjoyed the comradery and feeling of "family" in Doc's restaurant.

One of the things that struck me was that Doc never treated any employee as expendable. In fact, Doc acted as if you were going to be working with him for the rest of your life (although the restaurant industry typically has many part timers and high turnover). That commitment to people impressed me as a young manager and later in my career, influenced my business philosophy.

After completing college and moving to the community where we wanted to raise our family, I accepted a Human Resources Manager position in a local manufacturing company. Unfortunately, that company regarded employees as "commodities" that they hired and replaced as necessary. It wasn't that the company necessarily mistreated people but there was certainly no interest in employees' lives nor was there any commitment to them. Following a significant downturn in business I was charged with laying off nearly 200 employees. Speaking to each employee one-on-one, I witnessed the fear they felt. I heard their stories and I saw their tears. How would they pay their bills? How would they feed their families? At the end of the day I would come home emotionally drained and when all the layoffs were finally announced I experienced an anger over what I considered was a complete failure of management to prevent this. I vowed that to the extent I could have something to do about it, I would never go through this again.

In my next management position, while our team was developing our strategic marketing plan, I learned about the Customer Intimate marketing model. This intrigued me as it promoted customers for life and fit our company's direction. As I thought about Doc and how he committed himself to people, I explored the idea of establishing a value which espoused **Customers for Life**, **Suppliers for Life** and **Employees for Life**.

The management team easily accepted the proposal to target specific companies who would be a good fit for our products and services, provide them exceptional service and augmented programs, partner with them and value them as **Customers for Life** (the Customer Intimate Model).

The value of **Suppliers for Life** however, took more consideration by the management team. Not all suppliers were worthy of that designation. There were, however, a number of key suppliers who, with special partnering initiatives over time, did qualify as Suppliers for Life. The benefits from these relationships were unquestionable and we eventually adopted the **Suppliers for Life** value.

*What did **Employees for Life** mean to us? Certainly, we had no contracts with employees. They could come and go as they pleased. And the company could hire and dismiss employees as it pleased. But my interest stemmed from what I had seen while working with Doc. His genuine concern for people and the time he spent with them created in his employees a connection that transcended the usual employer/employee relationship. There was trust. There was sharing. There was sacrifice. These things didn't just happen. Closeness like this was cultivated over years of employee relationships.*

*Was there a mutual benefit to this value? Absolutely. The jobs within our company had become increasingly technical and the training times were eighteen months or longer. The cost of any turnover was too penalizing. From the employees' points of view, the company was located in a small community with few other opportunities for work without lengthy commutes. Employees wanted the stability of a company they could count on. The company needed well-trained long term employees. We needed each other. From this came the proposed value of **Employees for Life**.*

*What did **Employees for Life** mean? It meant that we would invest in employees for the long term. Training programs, benefit packages, communications, etc. were all geared toward the assumption that this was the last place employees were going to work. Our hiring practices were stepped up to include profiles to help us identify those who would most likely be successful in these positions. We established internships where new employees were paid to attend technical training – courses we developed in conjunction with the local technical college. And most visibly, we announced that we were a "no lay off company." We committed to running our company in such a way that we could weather the ups and downs of the market without laying off employees.*

So what did we do when business was down? We did three things:

- ✓ We improved our workplace organization and cleanliness. We cleaned, we painted and we organized.
- ✓ We cross-trained. Each operator had the goal of learning two other positions and becoming proficient in them.
- ✓ We became trainers for others. Employees attended courses on how to train others and took on the responsibility to become certified trainers for new employees and existing employees who wished to be cross-trained.

We emphasized that being a "no layoff company" did not mean that our company was a safe haven for everyone, but that it stressed the importance of each of us holding our own and improving in our performance standards.

One of the first major opportunities for us to demonstrate our commitment to our **Employees for Life** *value was when the industry experienced a significant downturn for about 18 months. The management team took on responsibilities to tighten our belts in all areas without any reduction in workforce or hours. Also, we agreed that while we would hold the line on raises, improvement in job skills would still qualify for pay increases. Employees shifted to workplace organization and training initiatives.*

During this time, our competitors laid off many of their employees and shut down some of their operations. We, however, held firm to our plan – and still remained profitable. It was not without sacrifice, however, and the "values in action" I saw endeared me to the management team forever. Part of the team's pay was tied to financial performance and with the decline in business without a corresponding reduction in work force, the management team's goals were not going to be met. We talked about this and agreed that we would all take a "hit" during this time, to be able to support our no layoff policy. We also talked about and prepared employees for what we anticipated would be an opportunity for the company to experience rapid growth when the market came back.

Why did we think we would experience rapid growth? Because we recognized that our competitors, who had laid off their employees and shuttered their plants, would not be able to respond quickly to a market comeback. It takes time to start up a plant that's been shut down. It takes time to recall employees and some don't ever return. Those who do return have trust and fear issues about their job security. Productivity is generally low following a recall to work. Our thoughts were that when the market geared up, we would experience a "slingshot" effect – and we prepared our employees for it so when it came, we would go into overtime mode, produce products with very short lead times and gain many new customers. And that's what happened. Our growth rate when the market came back was phenomenal and our competitors could not respond to all the requests from customers. But we could and we did.

*The unselfish sacrifice of the management team to individually take a cut in their pay in order to support the value of **Employees for Life** was commendable.*

The rest of the story: the company's growth and improvement in bottom line performance resulted in bonuses for the management team that more than made up for their previous loss. I was never more proud of the team for what they did.

In future chapters you will see more examples of how the values of a company affect the strategic business planning process, the marketing strategy and most other business decisions.

As a business leader, it's your responsibility to declare, teach and live your values. As the writer in Proverbs states, "I instruct you in the way of wisdom and lead you along straight paths." Proverbs 4:11

Business / Life Principles in Proverbs

The Book of Proverbs has a great deal to say about how one should conduct his or her life. Here are some examples.

On honesty and integrity...

"The Lord abhors dishonest scales, but accurate weights are his delight." *(11:1)* "Ill-gotten treasures are of no value..." *(10:2a)* "Dishonest money dwindles away..." *(13:11a)* "A fortune made by a lying tongue is a fleeting vapor and a deadly snare" *(21:6)* "...he who hates ill-gotten gain will enjoy a long life" *(28:16b)* See also 15:27a; 19:22b; 20:17

On hard work...

"He who tends a fig tree will eat its fruit..." *(27:18)* "Lazy hands make a man poor, but diligent hands bring wealth." *(10:4)* "He who works his land will have abundant food, but he who chases fantasies lacks judgment." *(12:11)* "As vinegar to the teeth and smoke to the eyes, so is a sluggard to those who send him." See also 21:25-26; 30:15; 20:13

On wise planning...

"The plans of the diligent lead to profit as surely as haste leads to poverty." *(21:5)* "Ants are creatures of little strength, yet they store up their food in the summer..." *(30:25)* "In his heart a man plans his course, but the Lord determines his steps" *(16:8)* See also 6:6-8; 20:4; 27:23-24

On procrastination...

"He who gathers crops in summer is a wise son, but he who sleeps during harvest is a disgraceful son." *(10:5)* "All hard work brings a profit, but mere talk leads only to poverty." *(14:23)*

On generosity...

"A generous man will prosper; he who refreshes others will himself be refreshed." *(11:25)* "He who is kind to the poor lends to the Lord, and he will reward him for what he has done." *(19:17)* "One man gives freely, yet gains even more; another withholds unduly, but comes to poverty. A generous man will prosper; he who refreshes others will himself be refreshed." *(11:24-25)*

Chapter 4
Customer Focused Business Plan

Before you launch out on any venture, you need to have a plan. In this chapter you will learn a simple approach to creating a business plan - one that focuses on your customers - therefore, the title "Strategic Customer-Focused Business Plan."

Business owners sometimes lose focus on whom they are serving - and that's a serious error. Business planning should take in what the customer needs, where you are strong in meeting those needs (and where you need to shore up your offerings) and how to prioritize your objectives and action plans to meet your customers' needs.

This chapter also has an application for your personal life. As you plan for your family's future, consider where your strengths are. Consider what your weaknesses are. Focus on what your family's real needs are.

Remember Jesus' words: "Where your treasure is, there your heart will be also" (Matthew 6:21).

Love,
Dad

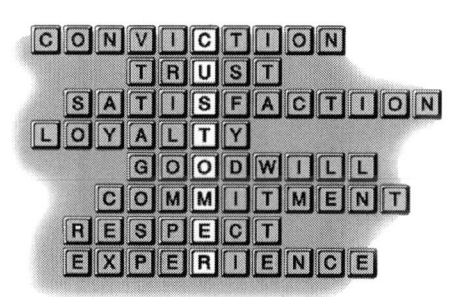

CONVICTION
TRUST
SATISFACTION
LOYALTY
GOODWILL
COMMITMENT
RESPECT
EXPERIENCE

Strategic Customer-Focused Business Plan

The process of Strategic Business Planning is very involved. It begins with your management team looking at the market your company serves, focusing intensely on what the market's needs are (especially the unmet needs – the opportunities). It then looks at the capabilities you bring to the market – where you're strong and where you're weak. These capabilities not only include the basic operational skill sets necessary to be successful, they also address facilities, equipment, personnel and financial strength - every facet of an organization that is critical to the success of the business.

Your strategic business plan serves as a template for your organization's direction (it engages your vision, mission and values) and becomes a baseline to see how well you are performing. From this planning process you will create company objectives, action plans and milestones. Your mission will become much more defined and you will use your business plan to communicate frequently to employees the WHAT, WHY, and HOW of your business.

Your approach should be this: *"If we follow the plan, we will achieve success."* As you review your progress and your plan, you will make changes as needed, learning as you travel down your mission road. Review your plan at least annually (with brief reviews quarterly). Your Strategic Business Plan should normally go out three years, with very specific details for year one. In some cases companies will look out as long as five years, depending on the markets they are serving.

> Note: A Strategic Business Plan differs from your financial business plan, which is much more detailed and provides analysis and strategies for financing your growth. Example: your banker will want to see your Strategic Business Plan but will also require a review of your financial business plan.

The following is a very basic review of the strategic business planning process and is certainly adequate for most small businesses. Should you wish to create a more detailed plan, a good on-line resource is PlanWare (www.planware.org).

Preparing for the Strategic Planning Process

Schedule 3-4 half day sessions with your management team. Ensure that all managers attend all sessions, even if it requires rescheduling. Ownership of the process is crucial to your planning success.

Materials needed: adhesive flip chart paper, wall space to post charts, broad tip markers.

Session 1

1. Review the reasons for creating your Strategic Business Plan and the importance of each manager's participation and the team's ownership. Explain how the plan will be communicated to employees and how it will serve as a performance measurement tool for the company.

2. Stress the need for the team to be candid and free in their remarks, yet respectful of differences. Share that the team will work toward consensus in all key points.

3. Conduct a SWOT Analysis

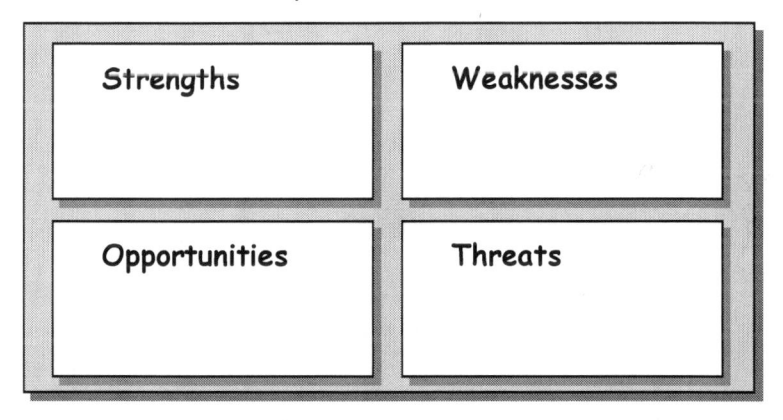

Strengths	Weaknesses
Opportunities	Threats

4. After drawing this chart on the wall, share how the SWOT Analysis is a useful management tool for revealing *internal* strengths and weaknesses and *external* opportunities and threats. Remind the team that each entry should be applicable to the market you are serving. Share a couple examples of each:
   - ✓ *"Our maintenance department's machine up time performance is outstanding. When we need to use our equipment, it works. We have very little down time."* **An internal strength**

- ✓ *"Our computer systems are outdated and cause us occasional productivity problems."* **An internal weakness**
- ✓ *"Due to environmental concerns, demand for our industry's products is expected to increase in the next three years."* **An external opportunity**
- ✓ *"New OSHA regulations will require us to make an investment in equipment and training."* **An external threat**

5. State the primary function of your business (e.g., "We provide pollution control equipment to municipalities and regulatory agencies in North America").

6. Now, ask the managers to share the strengths they feel the company has in order to serve your customers (remember, this is a customer-focused plan). While you will start with naming your internal strengths, as you hear of an external opportunity, log it accordingly. Do the same with comments regarding internal weaknesses and external threats. Continue to go round and round with the managers until you are convinced that you have exhausted their input.

The Importance/Performance Matrix

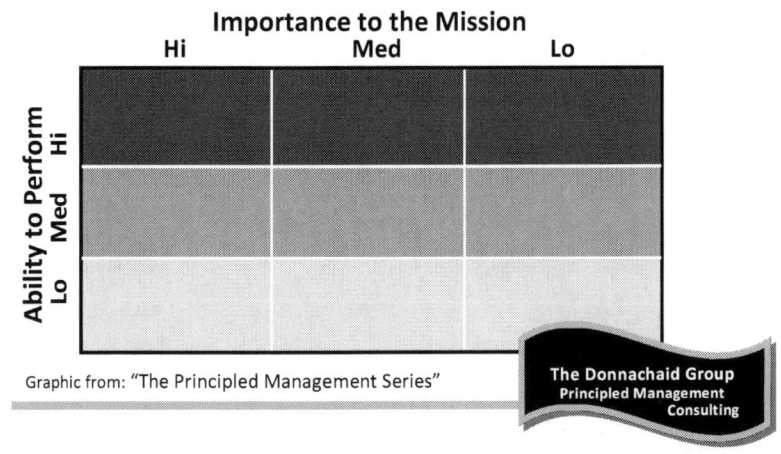

Importance to the Mission: Hi / Med / Lo

Ability to Perform: Hi / Med / Lo

Graphic from: "The Principled Management Series"

The Donnachaid Group
Principled Management Consulting

7. Draw the above **Importance/Performance Matrix** with your core mission statement across the top of the chart. As in the following example, write "**Providing pollution control equipment to municipalities and regulatory agencies in**

Legacy - Principled Management   Customer Focused Business Plan - 41

North America." On the left side of the matrix write "**Ability to Perform**." Explain that the team will now place each of the entries from the **SWOT Analysis** on this chart. Note: for ease in doing this, you may wish to number the individual strengths, weaknesses, opportunities and threats so that you are only entering the corresponding number of each item.

8. For each item, ask, *"Considering our mission to provide pollution control equipment to municipalities and regulatory agencies in North America, where should we place _____? Is it of high importance, medium importance or low importance?"* Once the team has determined this, then ask, *"And what's our ability to perform? Is it high, medium or low?"* Don't allow the dialogue to get too involved, rather, ask for gut responses and brief clarification. It is important that there is consensus on the opinions but it is not too important to distinguish, for example, between a "medium-high" vs. a "low-high."

9. Once you have plotted all the items, draw a straight line from the lower left-hand corner of the chart to the upper right-hand corner; then bisect the upper left triangle by drawing a line from the upper left-hand corner to the mid-point of the line you previously drew.

Your focus will be on those items on the left side of the chart (see example below) and your next step will be to set priorities on each of these items. End this session, encouraging the management team to look forward to the next session's work.

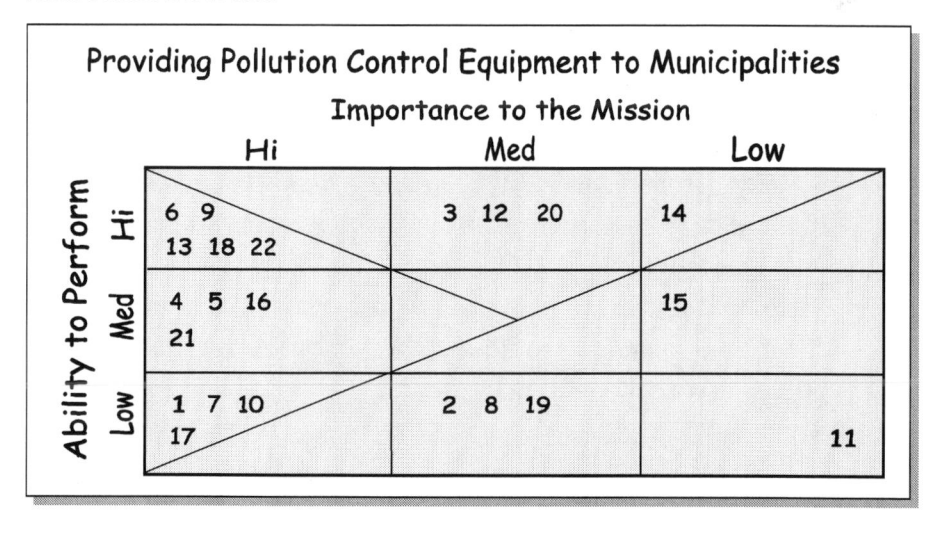

Providing Pollution Control Equipment to Municipalities

Importance to the Mission

Ability to Perform	Hi	Med	Low
Hi	6 9 13 18 22	3 12 20	14
Med	4 5 16 21		15
Low	1 7 10 17	2 8 19	11

Session 2

1. Review what was accomplished in session 1 and ask if there are any questions. Note: all of your work from the first session should be posted on the walls.

2. Refer to your completed **Importance/Performance Matrix**. Seek the team's understanding of why, when you drew the lines as you did (see example), you only need to focus on those items in the triangle on the left. For example, if item 11 was *"Our office chairs are getting worn,"* discuss how buying new office chairs cannot be seen as terribly important to the mission and, in light of all the other items that are important to the mission, the company's *"ability to perform"* is very low – there wouldn't be enough left in the budget to make the purchase. Once you feel the team understands, then move on to the next step.

3. Starting with the lower left hand side of your matrix, explain that the team's priority begins with those items, moving up the chart. For example, #17 is highly important to your mission but your ability to perform is very low. This means that #17 becomes one of your top objectives on your action list. What would be the next items? Answer: #1, #7 and #10, then #21, etc.

   As you create your action plans, the actions you assign to the items at the top change in their scope. For example, if item #6 is *"Our customer service personnel are highly trained and responsive to customer phone calls and e-mails,"* then the management team's action may be to sustain customer service performance and create a training program for new customer service personnel. Accordingly, this action will have a lower priority than other action items.

Legacy - Principled Management Customer Focused Business Plan - 43

Create your Action Plan with Smart Objectives

Action Plans - Objectives

Objective	Who	When	What "success" will look like
Create a price list that is within 10% of the competition	Joe Adams	By 4/22	A price list, with columns noting the top three competitors' pricing, by comparable product, and our proposed pricing (within 10% of the average competitor price)

When Creating Objectives, Think

"SMART"

Specific
Measurable
Attainable
Realistic
Timely

Graphic from: "The Principled Management Series"

The Donnachaid Group
Principled Management Consulting

4. For each item, write a SMART objective to put on your Action Plan list. SMART stands for: **S**pecific - **M**easurable - **A**ttainable - **R**ealistic - **T**imely. See the example above. A great question to ask, when writing an objective, is *"What will success look like?"*

5. Take your time writing your objectives. Seek out the primary manager who will be responsible for the completion of the objective. That manager's comments carry more weight than others, yet you still need to have the management team's consensus on these. When you've completed the list, copy each manager and ask them to take a week to review these to ensure that they are appropriate, that they are achievable in the time frame allotted and that the managers have the resources necessary to complete these.

Session 3

1. Confirm that each manager supports the objectives on your Action Plan list and that they can commit to their timely completion. Ask if any additional resources are needed. If they are, as the business leader you should commit to providing those resources. If you cannot do this, you should modify the objective.

2. Share with the management team that these objectives will be included in their performance reviews and will make up a significant part of their reviews. Be sure to announce the frequency of updates you require from each manager on each objective.

3. Assign the managers the task of creating a presentation for the company on their objectives and jointly plan a company event where you and all the managers will present the Strategic Business Plan to employees, followed by individual department meetings headed by department managers.

4. Reinforce that this is the team's plan - and if they work the plan, the company will achieve its goals.

Post-meeting work by business leader

Following the meeting, create a tracking program for each objective, charting the progress until completed. There are a number of stock programs you can use. Finally, consider what recognition and/or reward you will give for successful completion of each objective.

Chapter 5
Strategic Marketing & Sales Plan

- The Difference Between "Big M" and "small m" Marketing
- Marketing Models
- Distinctive Competencies
- A Simple Marketing Approach That Works
- Building Your Strategic Sales Plan from Your Strategic Marketing Plan
- Customer Relationship Management
- Measuring the Immeasurable – Customer Satisfaction

There is probably nothing more exciting in business than to experience a successful marketing plan bringing in opportunities for new customers. I was so fortunate to have learned from the writings of some of the best marketing minds – and then to have actually experienced the continued success of a marketing strategy.

As the management team grasped the importance of marketing, throughout the company employees began to connect with the work they were doing. They saw that they were the reason for the company's distinctive competencies and that those distinctive competencies were what the company was known for in the marketplace.

Knowledge of and appreciation for business principles, the value people put on business systems, and recognition for the importance of performance measurements all blossomed once people began to understand the company's strategic marketing.

Remember: to be valued, you must provide value. Marketing presents value to the marketplace in such a way that opportunities for new and continued business growth abound. It's exhilarating and something I hope you are privileged to experience.

Love,
Dad

Strategic Marketing & Sales Plan

> *"Marketing and innovation produce results; all the rest are costs. Marketing is the distinguishing, unique function of the business."* Peter Drucker

You've heard people refer to "Sales & Marketing" as a business function but that's really the wrong order of things - it's "Marketing," then "Sales." You cannot have sales without first having someone who wants to buy your product or service - and the way in which customers are informed of the *possibility* that you can meet their needs is through your marketing. Applying this definition, everything starts with marketing. Allow me to explain.

After creating your vision, mission and values, the most important work you and your management team will do is to create your strategic marketing and sales plan. And real work it is. Your team will be asked to state what the competencies of the company are and will be required to back up their statements with proofs. They will study and chart the sales process and learn about relationship development. Your management team will learn that marketing and sales is a science requiring several disciplines – it's not just something that *happens*.

Most of all, you will need to ask your team to set aside their predispositions and labels concerning marketing and sales – because *most of them will be wrong*. Don't be surprised that managers don't differentiate between marketing and advertising. Don't be surprised to feel resistance to adopting a *process approach* to sales. Few have been schooled in the science of marketing and sales and even fewer make the connection to its value - sadly including some who are in sales professions.

This is not an exhaustive study by any means; in fact it's at the tree tops level. Strategic Planning with the management team often takes months to accomplish and the use of a trained facilitator is recommended. In the next sections I will share some of the decisions you will need to make as you go through this process.

> *"Marketing is everything!"* - Bill Hannon, Compass Consulting

The Difference Between "Big M" and "small m" Marketing

In most circles when the term *marketing* is used, people are referencing catalogs, promotional programs, radio ads, lead generation activities, etc. These operational activities are tactical and are called "small m" marketing. For example, these tactical activities support the objectives you created in your SWOT Analysis and Importance/Performance Matrix exercise. These are the things that your staff employs *after* you have developed your strategic marketing and sales plan. And most importantly, *all* of your "small m" marketing activities flow from your "Big M" Marketing Plan. While we will be covering a few "small m" activities in *Legacy*, our primary focus will be on "Big M" Marketing.

What do I mean by "Big M" Marketing?

First of all, you can distinguish between "Big M" Marketing and "small m" marketing this way: "Big M" Marketing is about your business strategy:

- M *what* you're going to sell
- M *who* you're going to sell to
- M *how* you're going to position your company
- M *who* you are - and therefore, who you are *not*

In your strategic marketing planning, you will need to identify the following:

- M the primary product and/or service you offer the market
- M how the market purchases these products/services
- M who the buyers are in that market and where they are located
- M what the basic needs of that market are
- M who the current suppliers of this market are
- M what your market share is and what your competitors' market share is
- M whether your offerings are considered "commodities" or unique – and why

- **M** define your customer base and what they think of you – and how you know this
- **M** identify any "categories" or "distinguishers" that exist in this market:
  - ✓ based on quality and performance of the product or service
  - ✓ based on price of the product or service
  - ✓ based on added-value uniqueness of the product or service
  - ✓ based on distribution of the product or service
  - ✓ based on well known "brands"
  - ✓ based on patents or trade secrets
  - ✓ based on unique obstacles to market that may exist
  - ✓ based on regulatory agencies and/or approvals that apply

When you have done this, you and your management team will need to go back to your vision and mission and define how you want to see your company performing in this market in the future. This should include:

- **M** choosing the most appropriate marketing model(s) for your business
- **M** identifying unique needs that you could meet, to differentiate you from your competitors
- **M** identifying the geographic market you will serve
- **M** defining your "value proposition" - what you bring to the market
- **M** describing the image you wish to portray

When speaking of "Big M" Marketing, consider that once you have developed your Strategic Marketing Plan, *everything* else in the company will flow from this. I'm not just speaking of sales, although your Strategic Sales Plan will certainly flow from your Strategic Marketing Plan. I'm declaring that *every other functional department in your company* will take its cue from your Strategic Marketing Plan and will be subservient to that plan.

"Big M" Marketing defines who you are, what you do, who you serve, how you serve them and how the entire company rallies around this to make it happen. Marketing truly is everything.

Legacy - Principled Management   Strategic Marketing & Sales Plan - 49

Marketing Models

Let's briefly review the three basic Marketing Models, as defined by Micheal Treacy and Fred Wiersema:

- **Operational Excellence**
- **Product or Technical Leadership**
- **Customer Intimacy**

What are these three models all about? Let's start with **Operational Excellence**. Companies who adopt an Operational Excellence Model as their primary discipline focus on Efficiency. They make it easy to do business with them and they're generally the low cost leader. Examples include Wal-Mart, McDonalds, and FedEx.

These companies focus on high volume, low cost, and invest in automation and systems to keep their costs as low as possible. Where they can't do that, they import from countries where the labor costs are very low.

What you see with an **Operational Excellence** model:

- e-commerce sites
- minimal sales force
- low cost supplier status
- lower margins
- efficiency, efficiency, efficiency
- not a lot of choices - no customization

"You can have any color you want... as long as it's black"
Henry Ford

The next model is called **Product Leadership** or for service and design companies, **Technical Expertise**. This approach applies when you are *the* company the market thinks of when it has a specific need. At one time you may recall that Xerox had this position, so much so that people used to say, *"make me a Xerox"* when they meant *"make me a photocopy."*

Product Leadership companies invest in the newest of technology. They're generally very entrepreneurial and ground-breaking in their business strategies and most are engineering-driven, seeking patents and trademarks, etc. A few examples you might recognize are Johnson & Johnson, W.L. Gore (the makers of GORE-TEX®), and Strauss Skates (you'll know them if you're a hockey player).

What you see with **the Product Leadership** or **Technical Expertise** model:

- industry "experts" on staff
- innovation and technical "proofs"
- secrecy agreements
- custom products/custom programs
- higher risk/higher margins

The third model is **Customer Intimacy**. With this model companies develop *"customers for life."* If you are a **Customer Intimate** company, you know your customers' needs very well and you adopt the value of "helping your customers succeed." Since you can't be all things to all people, you often find referrals, partnerships, etc. with the **Customer Intimate** model so even when you can't serve a customer, you find someone who can.

Of the big name companies, Nordstrom and Marriott are well known for adopting **Customer Intimate** models but I contend that there are hundreds of small businesses who do this, even if they're not consciously aware of having adopted such a model.

What you see with the **Customer Intimacy** model:

- a highly trained, empathetic sales force
- well staffed to serve customers
- the support of a well developed CRM system
- a complex relationship development system
- a longer, very involved sales cycle
- loyalty programs

> So, which model are you?

Operational Excellence? Unlikely, unless you're like Wal-Mart or McDonalds - although you can certainly put an emphasis on systems management, cost reductions and other efficiencies - and you should.

Product Leadership or **Technical Expertise?** Maybe, but certainly it's a limited model for most of us who don't own a patent on a unique technology nor do most of us have a department of engineers to develop new inventions. You may however have an employee who is highly knowledgeable in a particular area of expertise and each of us can and should have the highest measure of expertise that we can achieve in our particular field.

For most small businesses that leaves **Customer Intimacy**, the model most companies should consider as their primary marketing model. This is because small businesses, particularly those in a small town, have certain competitive advantages that their larger competitors – those with the efficiency marketing models – cannot offer to the local market. What are the advantages of being in a small town market? Let's explore them:

1. You know your customers personally (or have the opportunity to get to know them).
2. You have the opportunity to demonstrate your values in your business and your personal life.
3. You're a "local"- people can count on you being here.
4. Your reputation is fairly well known in the community.
5. Your transportation costs are low.
6. Your labor costs are generally more competitive.
7. You can develop generational relationships. When you build a relationship with a customer, you often build an ongoing relationship with their children and grandchildren (or at least you have that opportunity).
8. You can be a "big frog in a small pond." You don't have to worry about the national market - just your local market share.

More small town business owners should explore these competitive advantages and build them into their Strategic Marketing Plans.

A final note: Treacy and Wiersema contend that all companies need to be proficient in at least one of these models and at parity in the other two models. So if Customer Intimacy is your primary model, you still need to have a measure of proficiency in Technical Expertise and Operational Excellence.

Distinctive Competencies

What are distinctive competencies? They are:
- those attributes in your products and/or services that your customers recognize as *unique* and *desirable*
- generally something your competitors do not offer
- often why your customers buy from you

Examples of distinctive competencies:
- shortest lead times
- easy to use
- no minimum order size
- quickest service
- custom colors
- easy return policy
- custom designs
- informed staff
- life time guarantee
- real time order status
- always works
- quick ship capabilities
- strong relationships
- on time deliveries

So you think you have a distinctive competency? Prove it!

Building your business around distinctive competencies is a simple market strategy but it's also a lot of work. You will need to:

1. find out what your local market's needs are,
2. create your distinctive competencies, and then
3. align your people, processes, equipment, materials and systems - your entire organization - to support these offerings.

Become known in your local market for your competencies. Just as your values become part of your company's culture, engrain your distinctive competencies into your company's culture.

How do you do that?

1. You implement *measurements* (distinctive competencies are always measured).
2. You set *objectives* for continuous improvement.
3. You create *proofs* of your distinctive competencies.
4. You implement an effective *recognition and rewards program* to support this.
5. You incorporate *stories* of the company's distinctive competencies into your communications.

I emphasize the importance of **Distinctive Competencies** in marketing because they are the essence of your ability to be unique from your competitors.

A Simple Marketing Approach That Works

So, if you've never had an effective strategic marketing plan, where do you start?

A simple approach that works is to start by identifying **what your local market is not getting – or not getting very well** - and then, align your people, your processes, your equipment, your materials, your systems - your *entire organization* - to support providing these products and services to the market. Of course the latter part of this approach is not so simple. In fact, it's what separates routine businesses from unique businesses.

After several successful years of capturing an unmet niche in a market, I began to wonder why our competitors hadn't gone after this as well. The truth was, it was just plain too much work! To serve this particular niche we had to re-educate ourselves, we had to change our attitudes about what we were doing, we had to reorganize our production and we had to retrain our sales force. None of our typical pricing models worked - they all had to be created. On top of that, we couldn't experience turnover or we'd lose the specialty training we'd invested in our production staff. Our competitors didn't enter this market opportunity because it was too much work. In their eyes it wasn't worth it.

In our eyes however, we benefited greatly. We stretched our capabilities. We energized our work force. We felt we could do anything. And to reinforce the marketing plan direction, from the fruits of their labor - an improved bottom line - everyone received bonuses!

So once you've actually identified those market opportunities where customers are not being served, your challenge will be to walk through every operation in your company and assess what it will take to align your company to be able to provide these products and services and then confirm the following:

- Is this opportunity REAL...?
- Can we WIN...?
- Is it WORTH it...?

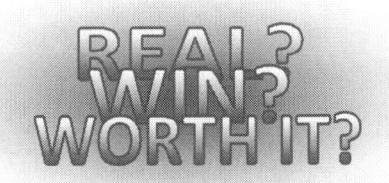

Created by Don Schrello, "Real-Win-Worth it" is used by many Fortune 500 companies to assess new products. While developing marketing strategy can be as complicated as you want to make it, the reality is that it can be as simple as finding something others are not doing – something the market needs – and creating the distinctive competency in your company to be able to reliably and repeatedly provide it. Of course, you must ensure that you can capture enough revenue from this venture to make the whole process worth it.

Remember that it's critical to get your management team behind your marketing plan and for your employees to really understand how important your distinctive competencies are to its success. The theorem that speaks to this is:

"A knowledgeable, committed team, embracing a commonly held set of values and vision, focused on a singular mission, under stress, will accomplish great things."

To implement a successful strategic marketing plan, you must educate your employees and connect your values and principles with what they do. And you need your employees to embrace these distinctive competencies as their own.

How do you do that?

Well, I'm a big believer in repetition. One of my mentors used to say,

"When you have something you want people to know, say it once, say it twice, say it over and over again until you think that everyone is sick and tired of hearing it - and then say it one more time!"

Once you've done that, have your employees say it back to you. In company meetings I would open by asking, *"What's the vision of this company?"* And then I'd ask, *"And what's the mission of this company?"* And then I'd follow that by quizzing, *"And what are our values, those guideposts that ensure we stay on the right path?"* And for each correct answer, there would be a prize given out. I did this every month for years.

In those same employee meetings, I would share the value of our company's distinctive competencies by making statements like:

"without this, here's where we'd be"

"our competitors cannot do what we do"

"our profitability and your pay are greater because of our ability to do this"

As a business leader, get good at telling stories and sharing examples and whenever you have the opportunity, demonstrate your company's values in action.

Building Your Strategic Sales Plan From Your Strategic Marketing Plan

Most companies know how to create a strategic sales plan utilizing the tactical actions of presenting their value proposition, providing literature and technical data, creating pricing structures based on sales volumes and/or customer relationships, employing sales staff inside and out in the field, creating sales call plans and logs, etc.

In *Legacy*, the emphasis is on ensuring that your strategic *sales* plan meets the objectives of your strategic *marketing* plan.

- You've identified the market you're serving: the customers, the products and services you'll be providing and the geographic territory you'll be working in. This is your "funnel", so to speak. Every opportunity that comes your way needs to make it through your funnel or be cast aside. Your strategic sales plan keeps your staff targeted in on prospects who meet your strategic marketing plan's criteria. The sales staff cannot be allowed to get pulled aside and waste resources chasing after things that are not part of the plan.
- Your customers and your definition of the "ideal customer" need to be profiled as to their typical organizational needs, so you can ensure you're meeting those needs.
- You then chart out the **sales cycle** for your staff, noting the steps that need to be taken throughout the timeline of the customer relationship development. Some companies have a relatively short sales cycle. Other companies have sales cycles that run 18 months or longer.
- From this needs analysis you build into your **sales cycle** specific actions for your sales staff to accomplish. Create a checklist as an easy way for reporting completion of these tasks. Examples include:

- Initial company introduction to Purchasing
- Product and service introduction
- Inquiries as to the customer's needs and concerns
- Confirmation of a likely "fit" between your two companies
- Visioning statements as to how a partnering relationship could be mutually beneficial
- Meeting with the Engineering Department
- Facility tour
- Meeting the Production staff
- Meeting the Receiving Department staff
- Meeting with the Quality Department staff and obtaining all relevant QA procedures
- Meeting upper management
- Inviting customer to visit your facility
- Digging into the personal needs of your immediate contact
- Sharing values and expectations (*"what we will do if..."*)
- Creating objectives and milestones
- Trial runs and samples
- Review of quality performance
- Review of relationship development

As you're looking at the possibility of growing your business, you have four basic options. Using the chart on the following page, you can conduct your own risk analysis on the best way to grow your business.

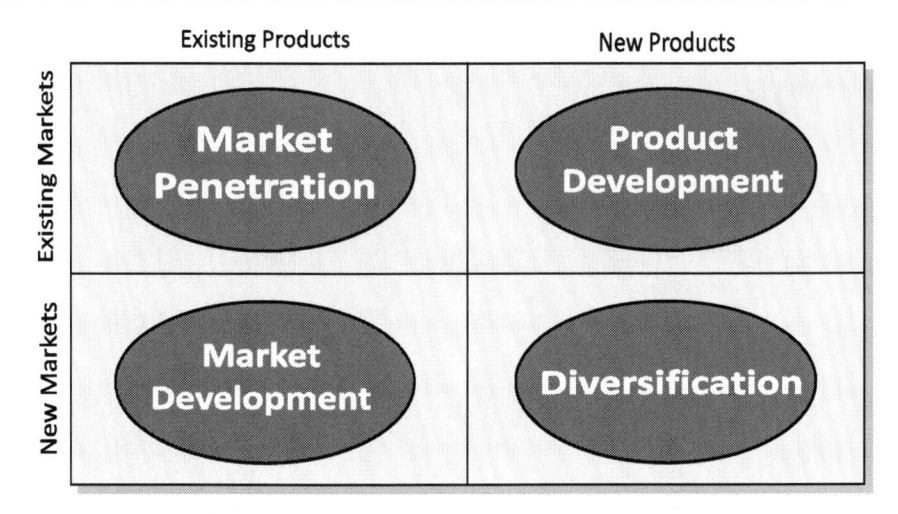

	Existing Products	New Products
Existing Markets	Market Penetration	Product Development
New Markets	Market Development	Diversification

- **Market Penetration**: This is simply a matter of selling more of what you currently offer to the same consumer group you currently serve (demographically, geographically, product-usage wise, etc.). This generally means outperforming your competitors and perhaps requires doing a better job of getting existing customers to increase their frequency of business with you.

- **Market Development**: If you consider that the best way to grow your business is to simply expand your geographic area - to sell the same products you're already offering to new customers - then your strategy should be to develop new markets (example: reaching out to surrounding communities). This strategy, called Market Development, requires you to grow the number of clients in your customer base while selling the same product lines you have.

- **New Product Development**: If you feel you have pretty much captured the number of customers in your local market and want to sell new and different products to them, then you implement the strategy of New Product Development. An example of this is a coffee shop that creates a new offering of gift baskets.

- **Diversification**: Finally, you always have the option of trying something completely different – selling completely new products/services to a completely new group of customers. This strategy is called Diversification.

> **Note**: You can also launch a combination of the first three marketing strategies but it will be very important to assess the risk of doing this.

Looking at these four Sales Growth strategies, the least risk is usually **Market Penetration**, simply selling more of what you are already selling in your same market area. This strategy makes the most sense when you know you're not getting as large a share of your local market as you should be getting. Your tactical marketing strategies should focus on convincing consumers to buy from you rather than your competitors - and/or to buy more often.

Market Development as a strategy depends heavily on what you are selling and whether customers are more likely or less likely to travel to buy from you. If attracting customers from a neighboring town is not an issue (examples: a dentist, a jeweler, shoe repair), then this is a very viable strategy.

If, however, you feel it's going to be difficult to convince people to travel those extra miles for your type of product or service (examples: fast food, coffee shop, gas station/car wash), then you should consider the **Product Development** strategy. Look at adding products and services that your existing customers will buy from you while they are already at your place of business. These are called complementary sales. Example: An oil change business should consider selling customers new windshield wiper blades.

The riskiest strategy of the four is clearly **Diversification** where you decide to approach an entirely new group of customers with a new offering of products and/or services that you've not sold before. If successful, however, the diversification strategy can provide you with a buffer (when one of your business sectors is down, another sector can shore up business). Example: A realtor who specializes in high end vacation homes (high margin, limited number of customers, highly sensitive to the economy) might diversify into opening a Subway restaurant (low margin, high volume business that holds up well in tough economic times). The risk? These are two very different businesses, requiring completely different management skill sets. It's why you often hear the business advice to "stick to knitting" - in other words, stick to what you know.

Customer Relationship Management

All relationships require nurturing. Consider the relationships in your personal life. You are closest to your immediate family and spend most of your time with them. They are your "inner circle." Further out in your circle are friends, aunts and uncles, cousins, acquaintances and distant relatives. The further out you go in your concentric circles, the less involved you are.

In Customer Relationship Management you recognize a similar set of concentric circles. You have premier customers you are very close to. Because of their volumes you're interacting with them almost daily and you get to know each other very well. And then there are good, but less frequent customers you serve. Finally, there are prospects whose business you are working on gaining so you are at the very early stages of developing a relationship with them.

In business, you have so many relationships. How do you keep them all vital and active? Don Peppers and Martha Rogers, authors of <u>The One to One Future: Building Relationships One Customer at a Time</u>, shared how the old neighborhood butcher would simply remember how his customer would like her favorite cut of meat. Because of a good memory and a great customer-focused attitude, he gave his customers personalized service. The limiting factor, of course, was the butcher's ability to remember everything.

In today's world of specialized software, we can easily "remember" those special tidbits of information through the use of a Customer Relationship Management program. The concept is simple: consider the types of information you want to remember and the program does the rest. My suggestion is to keep it simple. A simple CRM program that is *used* by your sales force is far better than a complex one that is *not used*. Here are some examples of information you may wish to collect:

- Business name, contact name, address, phone(s), fax, billing info, etc. (all the standard stuff).
- Markets they serve (products, services, geographic areas).
- Size of company in employees and dollar volume.
- What they are known for (their distinctive competencies).
- Key corporate initiatives.
- Promises made to the customer.
- Action plans in process and due dates.
- Percentage of business you have with them.
- Competitors who serve them and what percentage of business they have.
- Contact's birthday.
- Contact's anniversary.
- Contact's family info (spouse, children, where they go to school, etc.)
- Contact's hobbies and interests.
- Best time to call or visit.
- Contact's favorite food, restaurant, golf ball, etc.
- General info updates from sales calls.

Once this information has been entered into your CRM program, it's simply a matter of getting regular updates and new data entered in by anyone who interacts with the customer. You set alarms for all "to do" lists and annual recognition events (e.g., customer's birthday) to remind you to send a card, a gift, etc.

The rule is: do what you would normally do to develop a relationship with a customer - then program in the events and the activities to simply remind you. Continue to keep it personal (hand-signed notes, personal comments, etc.). While you can and should systemize the process, you should never drop the personal touch.

Measuring the Immeasurable
Customer Satisfaction

One of the more rewarding management tasks is to find out what your *customer* deems most important in your product and service offerings by rating you according to his or her priorities. It is a great way to find out where improvement is needed.

This section of **Legacy** covers a method of communicating with customers in such a way as to know you are doing what your customer expects and values. This Customer Satisfaction Measurement system also leads you in the creation of action plans and propagates your sales cycle activities.

The concepts behind measuring customer satisfaction were born out of a number of quality programs: the Malcolm Baldrige Award, ISO 9000, the Deming Prize, etc.

The struggle for most companies who launch customer satisfaction measurement programs is how to collect meaningful data. From my studies, I learned that the reliability factor associated with post card mail-back campaigns was so low that you'd be better off not doing anything. In recent years, there have been a number of on-line programs, however most of them do not provide for any customization by the customer. The customer is only allowed to answer the given questions and, other than the "additional comments" box at the end of the survey, there's no place for narratives.

No, if you want real meaningful feedback from your customers about how well you're serving them, there's one tried and true method for getting it. You simply ask!

In the following example, what you see is a simple template that lists . . .

- ***what*** performance items the customer chooses to rate
- ***how*** important each item is to the customer
- the ***rating*** on a scale of 1-10, with

    8 = "I received the products I expected"

    <8 = "I received less than I expected"

    >8 = "I received more than I expected"

- a **customer satisfaction score** (the weighting times the rating)
- the **total score**

What's unique about this method is that it

- allows the customer to decide what will be rated
- allows the customer to declare the level of importance of each rated item
- allows the customer to rate your performance on a scale that truly indicates satisfaction, dissatisfaction, or delight
- allows your customer to share the "why" of the above
- leads to an inarguable list of action plans, whose priority is set by the customer
- gives sales staff "assignments" and discussion points for future sales calls
- documents the process for others in both organizations to see
- promotes recognition and value for completed action plans in the following year's review
- facilitates data being grouped, by market, to identify trends
- provides a *quantitative* measurement to a *qualitative* process (what most companies struggle with in meeting Baldrige, ISO 9000, or other quality program requirements)

For large customers, the best method is to conduct this review at the customer's worksite, involving a cross section of their management team as participants lead by the account manager or a facilitator. For smaller accounts, a well-trained facilitator can successfully do this by phone. Phone evaluations should be scheduled in advance, with templates and instructions sent to the customer beforehand.

Customer Satisfaction Measurement

Ratings: 8 "I received the products and services I expected"
            <8 "I received less than I expected"
            >8 "I received more than I expected"

Customer's Name	Symbiotic Systems, Inc.
Address	123 Fourth Street
	Avon, Wisconsin 54755
E-Mail	sueb@symbiotic.com
Phone	555-123-4567
Date	11/12/13
Account Manager	John Gentry

Items Being Rated	A Importance To Customer	B Customer's Rating	C Customer's Satisfaction Score (AxB)	
Product Quality	20	8	160	
On-Time Delivery	15	7	105	
Lead Times	10	5	50	
Competitive Pricing	20	8	160	
Sales Support	10	9	90	
Business Relationship	10	8	80	
Technical Support	10	9	90	
Understanding Customer Business	5	6	30	
Total	100%	- - - - - -	765	

Action Plans: _____
_____
_____

Chapter 6
Information & Communication Systems

These two disciplines used to be separate, but with the growth of technology, Information Systems and Communication Systems are now often married together. Each serves the other, but both serve every department in the organization - which is an important distinction.

Unfortunately, we're in an age where we witness adults and children so engaged with their cell phones and PDA's that they are often addicted to them. As a business leader, it's important to realize that systems and technology serve us in doing our jobs better and more efficiently, but we must take care that we don't become slaves to the system. In the words of Star Trek's Mr. Spock, "Computers make excellent and efficient servants, but I have no wish to serve under them."

In this chapter we will review the necessary Information and Communication Systems for most businesses and how they can best serve management and the organization.

Love,
Dad

Information & Communications Systems

Information Technology (IT) and Human Resources (HR) serve every functional area of a company. They are the true "servant leaders" in the organization and business leaders need to be sensitive to the unique roles they play. Neither function would exist by itself. Both functions serve each other.

The unique commonality for both Information and Communications Systems is that *every functional area of your company must be competent in and integrate both disciplines.* Think about it. If you are the Maintenance Manager, you require Information Systems to integrate predictive maintenance. You also require Communications Systems to inform, educate and communicate with every member of your staff on all shifts, 24/7. You can do this same analysis for every department.

As we look at the Human Resources function, we clearly see that there are certain Critical Business Systems owned exclusively by HR (e.g., wage administration, sexual harassment/discrimination complaints, etc.). These are HR's and HR's alone. Can you imagine the chaos in an organization if every department created and administered these systems on their own?

Consider Information Systems. If you look at the Sales Department, you find IT's support of pricing software, CRM programs, product designs, bills of materials and so on. If the sales staff selected its own programs, how would IT ever coordinate them with manufacturing's needs on the floor? It simply wouldn't work.

No, HR must create, train, implement and oversee those Communications Systems that support the entire organization. And IT must do the same with the Information Systems that support the entire organization. But it's more than that.

HR and IT have the common responsibility for *assessing* the HR and IT competencies of all individuals in *every* department and creating training programs to bring them to the necessary skill levels. This is a critical responsibility that is not always seen nor appreciated by management. Why is this important? Because the HR Manager and the IT Manager are charged with planning for the company's future needs and ensuring that employees are achieving these competencies at the same pace (see the Principle of Pace).

The Principle of Interdependency is important to apply to the training roles of HR and IT. So often other department managers are much too dependent on HR and IT and fail to require their employees to become proficient in these disciplines. Their role is to teach others to become competent - not to enable dependency.

The process of implementing Information and Communications Systems is always fraught with problems. What can HR allow individual departments to do on their own - and in their own way? What will IT allow regarding the personal use of computers? Can you imagine the problems a company would experience if one department gave more raises to its employees than other departments? Do managers realize that if every employee downloaded large numbers of files on to their computers the company's servers could be overloaded?

Think of Information and Communications Systems as a "framework" which helps support the entire organization in its mission. Selecting good servant leaders in these disciplines will greatly aid your company's success.

Legacy - Principled Management   68

"Every manager should spend at least 5% of his or her time thinking. The remaining 95% of your time you can go about your business mindlessly. But you *should* spend at least 5% of your time reflecting on what you're doing and why you are doing it."

- Linc Duncanson

I think he's just kidding about the "mindlessly" part!

PRINCIPLED MANAGEMENT SEMINAR

Chapter 7
Human Resources Plan

When we talk of resources, most think of equipment, building and land. In so doing, most managers readily hold to the importance of routine care for these resources. We clean and lubricate machines. We paint our buildings and replace the roofs when needed. Farmers rotate crops to avoid depleting the soil. Yes, most managers know about the care of resources.

Prior to the creation of SHRM (Society for Human Resource Management), the "people" management function in business was typically called "Personnel Management" or the "Staffing Department" (where people were hired and fired). The emphasis was on the beginning or the ending of the employee/employer relationship.

As management began to see the importance of taking care of employees, there was a shift toward considering people as a resource. Companies began investing in training, career development, and wellness programs. They began treating people as valuable resources who needed routine care and maintenance.

The same principle applies to our personal lives but often we forget its importance. We wash our cars and routinely change the oil and filter, but neglect to schedule a weekly night out with our spouse. Our families are our "human resources" and blessings in life. They need and deserve loving care and "maintenance."

Hopefully, you'll apply some of the thoughts in this chapter to your life and create your own "human resources plan."

Love,
Dad

Human Resources Plan

The most important human resources planning business leaders should do is *organizational development*. What functions do you need in your organization? What level of skill do you require? What will be the make up of your management team? How will they work together?

As you develop your management team, keep this statement in mind:

"A knowledgeable, committed team, embracing a commonly held set of values and vision, focused on a singular mission, under stress, will accomplish great things." Linc Duncanson

There are a number of qualifiers in this statement. Let's look at each one:

A **knowledgeable** team: How does your team become knowledgeable? You *teach* them! And you set up an environment where they teach *each other*. Your team must commit itself to ongoing education.

A knowledgeable **team:** How do those working for you become a team? They work at it. Managers work with their employees as individuals with individual needs. They work with their employees as a team, allowing them to succeed and learn that the team's combined output is greater than the sum of their individual efforts. They reward their employees as a team for their team accomplishments so they see the benefit of teaming together. And, although it's difficult, they let go of those who do not subscribe to that philosophy. If not done, you will have a very difficult time developing a functioning team.

A knowledgeable **committed** team: How do you get your team to be committed? You accomplish this by vesting your team in the financial performance of the company. You do this by acknowledging their efforts and contributions and rewarding them fairly. It is very important that your team be committed to the mission of the company.

A knowledgeable, committed team, embracing a **commonly held set of values and a vision**: *Whose* values? Yours! *Whose* vision? Yours! And the vision and the values must be "commonly held." That is to say, everyone in the company subscribes to them. In fact, the action verb I prefer to use is *embracing*. You want your team to embrace these values and to embrace the vision of the company. When you embrace something, you hold it dear. You don't let it go. You treat it as something of great importance. A knowledgeable, committed team, *embracing* a commonly held set of values and a vision...

...**focused** on a singular mission: There are so many distractions in life that keeping everyone focused is vital. As a leader, you do this in many ways - by revisiting the vision, mission and values often in meetings, in conversations, in written communications and in recognition events. Note that your team must be focused on a **singular mission** - not multiple missions - not the company's mission *plus* the individual's mission. No, you want your team to focus intensely on the road they are traveling and as their leader, you need to occasionally remind them of that.

A knowledgeable, committed team, embracing a commonly held set of values and a vision, focused on a singular mission, **under stress:** Does that seem odd to include "under stress"? Stress is a good thing unless it is overwhelming. Consider how metal is strengthened by putting it under stress during processing so when it needs to hold up, it will. Consider military training which purposely puts trainees under stress so when they are in combat they hold up. What ways might a leader put his people under stress to develop them for high performance? Look at employee training programs in fast food chains. Employees are trained to handle the stress of lunch rush orders. Think of EMT's and how they are trained so that when they come upon an accident their actions are second nature. Look at jobs with deadlines. Look at the process of setting goals with deadlines. To grow, people need to be tried and tested - hopefully in non-crisis situations - so when they are in a crisis it becomes second nature. Robert Greenleaf, who authored, <u>On Becoming a Servant Leader</u>, describes stress as *"what makes life interesting by giving it its challenge."*

Finally, as a leader you need to recognize that all of these qualifiers have their basis in *measurement, recognition* and *reward* (read chapter 9: Performance Management). How do you know if your team is improving? You know by measuring their performance. You know by comparing their performance against previous performance and to the goals and milestones you've set in your mission statement. You know because you measure.

Human Resources Systems

I once conducted an HR audit on a company, reviewing over seventy policies and practices to determine where their gaps were. Human Resources management is all about systems and while we will only be covering a few of these in *Legacy*, I'd like to emphasize the importance of the *consistent application of procedures* in HR. Again, HR is all about systems.

Some believe that they have a *natural ability* to judge people in the interviewing process, for example. In my experience, that's simply not the case. Thorough candidate screening involves profiles, reference checks, physicals, drug/alcohol screening, credit checks and interviewing by managers who have been trained in that process. Some of the most presentable candidates (on the surface) I have interviewed have had appalling backgrounds and would certainly have been problem employees. HR is all about the *disciplined adherence to systems*. The following are examples of **Critical HR Systems**:

Hiring Process: From the recruiting process through employee orientation, this is a "checklist" system with a number of disciplines to be followed. No steps in the hiring process can be skipped over and HR can never be coerced into speeding up the process by doing so (something the management team must honor). One data point to judge as to the effectiveness of this system is the *90 day turnover rate* (was the candidate a good fit for the position?).

Training System: While generally not responsible for all the training in a company, HR is responsible for the development of the *training system template*. What is that? The training system template directs managers to state their training objectives and measure the effectiveness of their training. Typically, this involves a basic outline that is used by all managers for their functional skills training and departmental procedures. This also involves testing and often certification. HR is responsible for the tracking of all training in the company, noting the competency levels assessed by the managers for their direct reports.

Career Pathing System: Career development is another **Critical HR System**. Working with upper management, the future staffing needs of the company are projected. HR is responsible for managing the combination of developing employees within the organization as well as recruiting and hiring from outside the organization. Many companies will give preference to internal candidates (a policy I endorse) but that means that an effective career pathing and development program must be in place.

Career pathing is more than a program that offers promotion opportunities to employees. An effective Career Pathing Program profiles and tests individuals and then assesses the employee's potential for succeeding in his career choice. Once confirmed, the program identifies the gaps in their education and skills, maps out a path to close those gaps (generally supported by tuition reimbursement programs), submits the plan to management for approval and once approved, tracks the individual's progress.

Wage Administration System: Regardless of the type of wage program in an organization, HR has the responsibility to audit the system to ensure fairness and compliance (based on skill level, performance, seniority, market, etc.). These reports go to upper management along with recommendations for any changes.

Communications System: This responsibility is covered in chapter 6 and is often overlooked as a **Critical Business System**. *What* is communicated, *how* it is communicated, the *frequency* of communications, communications *training* for managers and judging the *effectiveness* of company communications is HR's responsibility.

Specific Technical/Legal Areas: This varies by industry but there are certain sensitive technical and/or legal areas in business that HR and only HR is to handle. Examples include sexual harassment complaints, discrimination complaints, oversight of accident investigations and injury case management, EEOC compliance, the employee disciplinary process, etc.

Two areas that many companies struggle with are **Corrective Action** and **Performance Reviews**. The following are simple examples of both:

Corrective Action Plan: When an employee is failing in a job function or has poor work behaviors, you should first confirm that the employee understands what his responsibility is and has been adequately trained to carry out that function. Once you have done that, if improvement is not seen, then corrective action is called for.

Many managers struggle with how to do this yet the most effective manner is to . . .

- simply state what the concern is,
- note when it happened,
- state what you are expecting,
- state when you are expecting it to be corrected, and
- inform the employee of the consequences if improvement does not happen.

The next page has an example of a Corrective Action Plan:

> RE: Bill Smith - 5/22/2013
>
> The issue is: You have been leaving your work station unstocked and unorganized at the end of your shift. This has made it difficult for John when he comes on his shift. This has happened 3 times this month.
>
> Expectation: Each of us is responsible for stocking our work stations and leaving them neat and in order for the next employee's shift. We rely on one another to do this.
>
> When this needs to be corrected: Beginning with your next shift.
>
> What are the consequences of repeated concerns with your work station organization: You will not be eligible for any potential raise for one year.
>
> Reviewed by Jim Taylor *Jim Taylor* 5/22/2013
>
> Reviewed and accepted by Bill Smith *Bill Smith* 5/22/2013

> *"Whoever disregards discipline comes to poverty and shame, but whoever heeds correction is honored."*
> Proverbs 13:18

Performance Reviews: The purpose of a performance review is to share your honest evaluation of your employee's work, noting specific examples. It's also an excellent time to tie in the employee's career pathing plan and progress, and solicit any suggestions or concerns that he may have. Note: I generally do not endorse doing a wage review at the same time as a performance review.

Here's a simple exercise that demonstrates to supervisors how to conduct an effective performance review. The supervisor is given the following fictitious scenario to respond to:

> "We will be opening a new facility and you will be the department supervisor. You get to choose the top three employees in your department who you want to take with you. Tell us who those employees are and why you are choosing them."

Supervisor:

"The first person I will take with me is Joe. He's my right hand man. If I need to be gone, I can rely on him to oversee things well. He always keeps his work station clean and orderly. His production performance and quality ratings always exceed standards and he's a delight to work with. Everyone sees Joe as one of the top employees in my department."

After listing two more employees that he would take with him, the supervisor is given a different decision to make:

"Unfortunately, when we go to this new facility the staffing levels will be less and you will not be able to take two employees from your department. Tell us who the two employees are who you will not be taking with you and why."

Supervisor:

"Well, as much as I hate to say it, I would not take Jim with me. He's had continuing production problems over the last several months due to not paying attention to details. I've had complaints from the shift supervisor about how he leaves his work station when he goes home and I've also had to talk to him about his attitude being less than desirable. Jim doesn't appear to be happy here and he certainly isn't putting in the effort to improve. I wouldn't take him with me."

After sharing who the other employee is and his reasons, we thanked the supervisor and made the following observation:

"You have just done an excellent job of doing a performance evaluation of your employees. It's obvious that you hold Joe in high regard and it's just as obvious that you have issues with Jim. What you've just shared with us and how you shared it is exactly what you should share with Joe and Jim in their performance evaluations. And another thing, if Joe is that good, you should make sure that you are paying him fairly. We don't want to lose him. As far as Jim goes, it looks like a Corrective Action Plan is in order. Good job!"

Why do managers complicate the performance review process and risk giving an ineffective review, possibly offending (certainly not motivating) their employees? The examples above are real scenarios and the supervisor's comments came from the heart. Hard to improve on that.

Recognition

The Human Resources Department needs to take the lead in modeling recognition within the company. The following examples share ways to do this throughout the organization.

Why is recognition important? It's important because all principled managers should truly value their employees and appreciate their contributions to the company and to them, personally. It should be seen as genuine gratitude for their service.

To be effective, all recognition needs to come from the heart. Any other motivation for showing recognition will easily be seen by others as manipulative and insincere and will be counterproductive.

Consider what almost every employee thinks about when he goes home at the end of the workday. Deep down, what does he want to be assured of? What does he want to share with his family about work? What is generally *always* important to him?

Answer: It's important that he knows he's done a good job. It's important that his work is recognized. It's important that he feels valued and appreciated for what he does. And guess what? These things are important to *everybody*!

What is the best recognition? The best recognition is that which is aligned with the company's vision, mission, values, objectives, and quality policy. Why is this important? Because it's what you're wanting to accomplish and it's reinforcing what you want to see more of.

"Recognize those behaviors you want to see more of."

- Be specific:

  "One of the things I appreciate about you, Sue, is your ability to level with me about issues. I always know where you stand."

- Be real (sincere, from the heart):

  "I realize that not everyone is that comfortable sharing their thoughts, but you are."

- Connect recognition with the company's values:

  "And when you do this, you've always been respectful, without dodging the issue."

- Show your appreciation:

  "Thank you, Sue."

HR starts by training others in the company how to give recognition and modeling this themselves:

- In orientations, communicate the value of recognizing others.
- Demonstrate the ways recognition can be given:
  - ✓ privately, one-on-one
  - ✓ in small groups (e.g., department)
  - ✓ publicly, in company-wide meetings
  - ✓ publicly, in newspapers & journals
  - ✓ special (such as sending a letter to the employee's spouse)

The following are some "tried and true" ideas (note the systems approach).

- Supervisors Daily "Walk About" (3 times):
  - ✓ at the start of the day, acknowledging the work that is in the schedule...

- ✓ midday, touching base on the basic measurables and commenting appropriately...
- ✓ at the end of the day, reviewing what was accomplished and thanking the employee for the day's work.

- Create an "iconic" award in your company. This can be a small statue or other object, particularly something that relates to your company. Give this award a name, create a chant or a song and use this for public recognition. Here is an example:

*"We're here today to stand and shout,
And you are what it's all about
'Cause what you did before our eyes,
Is what we want to recognize!"*

Have fun with this and encourage everyone to submit candidates for this award. Note: don't restrict this only to employees. Consider giving recognition to suppliers as well.

- Create an incentive compensation program (read chapter 10)...
  - ✓ that includes everyone in the company
  - ✓ that focuses on easy-to-understand measurables
  - ✓ that focuses on department or corporate objectives
  - ✓ that is measured and communicated at least monthly
  - ✓ that shares bottom line improvement
  - ✓ that ties the work that people do to results in profitability, productivity and quality

- Give recognition for loyalty & longevity
  - ✓ consider doing this for every 5 year milestone (5, 10, 15, etc.)
  - ✓ set a budget for each recognition
  - ✓ have a potluck luncheon where the company provides some basic food and employees bring their dishes

- ✓ tell stories that include achievements and acknowledge character
- ✓ ensure that supervisors, managers and top executives attend and have something to share (they should put an effort into this)
- ✓ invite the employee's family to attend
- ✓ videotape the event, set it to music and give a copy to the employee
- ✓ create a photo wall for all employees with more than 20 years

- Recognize continuing education and in-house technical advancement
  - ✓ conduct public recognition for promotions
  - ✓ provide framed certificates and a letter from the department manager
  - ✓ put employee recognition photos in the hometown newspapers where the company is located and also where the employee lives
  - ✓ connect the achievement with opportunity for advancement in the company

- Make "recognizing your employees" a management objective for each department manager with specific goals for...
  - ✓ learning how to give recognition
  - ✓ practicing this with department employees
  - ✓ keeping a record of who was recognized and why
  - ✓ reviewing the effectiveness of this with HR

- Birthday Cards

  The department manager and one or two top executives should make personal notes of appreciation in each card. This requires a simple system with an assigned person to select cards, hand address them, get them out to the managers ahead of time and mail them to the employee's home.

- Company Picnic

    Yes, picnics are a lot of work but what better way is there to have all of your employees, their families (especially the children), and friends all gather at the same place and at the same time. Old fashioned get-togethers are a perfect setting for your top executives and department managers to mingle around and to thank everyone for their contributions. Company picnics are well worth the effort.

- Send handwritten "thank you" notes. This seems to have become a lost art, yet few things are as powerful as a handwritten note of appreciation.

    ✓ Enter a weekly "task" in your scheduler to remind you to send these important thank you notes

    ✓ Invest in some personalized note cards

    ✓ Hand write your notes - *don't* type them

    ✓ Keep your foundational focus in mind as you write them

"...encourage one another and build each other up, just as in fact you are doing. Now we ask you, brothers and sisters, to acknowledge those who work hard among you, who care for you in the Lord and who admonish you. Hold them in the highest regard in love because of their work."

Chapter 8
Critical Business Systems

The red light on your dashboard that flashes "Engine Hot" is actually a warning system designed to signal you that immediate action is necessary to prevent damaging your car. This "dummy light" however, is not a failsafe system - it's only a warning indicator that something is wrong. The critical maintenance system that's documented in your vehicle manual includes oil change frequency and other checks to prevent the overheating of your engine.

The Critical Business Systems approach was developed as a failsafe for essential ISO 9000 operations. As you read this chapter, note that the focus is on the key operational functions of a business - those things that, if left unattended, could result in serious damage to your business. Ergo, they are deemed "critical."

Love,

Dad

Critical Business Systems

This topic is toward the end of **Legacy** for a reason - business leaders need to have a good understanding of the foundational building blocks to their businesses to appreciate the concept of Critical Business Systems.

This approach is closely tied to the requirements for certification to ISO 9000. To keep it simple you will first need to identify *all* the systems in your company that are responsible for the on time delivery of your product. This includes *every* operational function in every department. Each department has a "receivable" from its internal suppliers. Each has a "deliverable" to its internal customers. The Critical Business Systems approach requires you to recognize these *receivables* and *deliverables* and to focus your attention on the systems that produce them.

The Critical Business Systems approach involves defining the systems, creating and conducting audits, creating and implementing training programs, conducting value stream mapping of processes and risk assessment, analyzing performance measurements and planning for improvements.

Begin by conducting operational assessments of every function. Note: this is a significant initiative and commitment and is not to be taken lightly. The following are the steps to implementing Critical Business Systems in your company:

1. Meet individually with each department manager.
2. List the department's receivables.
    a. Ask the manager to describe the systems that are in place to ensure that these are:
        (1) provided as needed,
        (2) to your expectations,
        (3) on a timely basis.
    b. Ask what documentation exits.
    c. Ask what performance data exists.

3. List the department's deliverables.
   a. Ask the manager to describe the systems that are in place to ensure that these are:
      (1) delivered on time,
      (2) to your internal customer's expectations,
      (3) within cost projections.
   b. Ask what documentation exists.
   c. Ask what performance data exists.
4. Ask each department manager to identify all the systems that, if left unattended, could result in significant quality, delivery, scrap, cost, or safety issues - perhaps even "sink the ship" issues.
   a. Ask this question of department employees:

      *"If something were to go wrong in your area, **what** would that be and **how bad** would it be?"*
   b. Make a list of all comments.
      (1) When these issues arise, how do you fix them?
      (2) What is the frequency of these concerns?
      (3) Have there been any problem solving exercises to resolve these issues? If so, ask for documentation on what was done.
5. Working with the department manager, agree on what the department's 3-4 key critical business systems are.
6. If you are ISO 9000 certified, review the documentation for these systems.
7. If you are not ISO 9000 certified, create process documentation for each system. You may need assistance from your Quality Manager for this project to ensure consistency in format. Value stream map the process.

8. Create training programs for each system. See your HR Manager to ensure consistency and compliance to training formats.
9. Document the current performance.
10. Address the employee comments in 4a & b.
11. Assign a performance objective to the department manager to improve the performance of each system using problem-solving tools.
12. Assign the Quality Manager the task of creating and conducting audits of each department's Critical Business Systems and to work with each department manager on informal audits they should perform on a frequent basis.
13. Create an internal customer satisfaction measurement review to ensure that the department is delivering what its internal customer expects (note: this is similar to the satisfaction measurement system in chapter 5).
14. Communicate this initiative to the management team and to all employees. Update them frequently on departments' progress.
15. Repeat this process in each department until you've identified all Critical Business Systems in the company.
16. Include *"continuous improvement of the department's Critical Business Systems"* in each manager's performance objectives. Use value stream mapping as a tool to improve departments' processes and eliminate needless costs.

Once you have adopted and integrated this systems approach within your company, manage your progress utilizing Performance Management techniques. You and your management team will see how all the company's functions fit together.

The Critical Business Systems approach is a very effective management tool.

Chapter 9

Performance Management System

> Sometimes we forget the importance of simply treating people well and recognizing their value to others. While the study of Performance Management can be quite refined, the real beauty of this management philosophy is in its simplicity.
>
> Performance Management is a style anyone can practice. You just have to care about others. You just have to want to serve. You just have to be real.
>
> In your personal life, there are many things you can do to promote good relationships: setting a regular date night, having family dinners, and so on. These are simple things you can do and they're important to do. Keep that in mind as you read this chapter of *Legacy*.
>
> Love,
> Dad

Performance Management System

The definition of **Performance Management** is:

> *"A leadership methodology and style that connects management's expectations of each individual's work, on a daily basis, with the practice of recognition, reward and redirection – resulting in the reinforcement of the behaviors necessary for continuous improvement and the involvement of people who, when going home at the end of the day, all know how well they did."* Linc Duncanson

Aubrey Daniels is considered to be the "father of performance management." His consulting organization has worked with hundreds of companies worldwide teaching management teams the science of behavioral analysis. Adamant about continuous improvement, Aubrey Daniels contends that any objective can be measured and that the best people to record the measurements are the operators who perform the tasks.

Operators record their performance daily. Supervisors are taught how to appropriately respond to this performance, whether it is improved, stable or declining (see example below).

Performance Management requires that you look at *why* people behave as they do. It teaches you to recognize the behaviors that are in line with the company's objectives and to interact with your employees on a daily basis – three times per day – connecting these objectives with the work each employee is doing. Here's an example:

> *Supervisor Jim:* "Good morning, Ken. Looking at the jobs in front of you, it looks like you've got a busy day ahead. Is there anything you're concerned about with any of these orders?"
>
> *Ken:* "No."
>
> *Supervisor Jim:* "Great! What about the O'Henry job? That's given us a lot of problems in the past. Do you need any help need with that?"
>
> *Ken:* "I don't think so. I'm pretty sure I know what has to be done to eliminate the issues we experienced."

Supervisor Jim: "Well alright, let me know if there's anything I can do to help. By the way, before you leave today could I ask you to do an extra good clean-up on the computer keyboard and phone handset? There are a lot of colds going around and using those antiseptic wipes might help prevent someone from getting sick."

Ken: "No problem."

Supervisor Jim: "Thanks! I'll catch you later."

At midday, Jim swings by to informally check with Ken.

Supervisor Jim: "Hey, Ken. How are things going?" Jim sees that Ken is better than half way through and recognizes this by saying, "Looks like you're ahead of schedule. Good job! Anything I can help you with?"

Ken: "I could use some WD-40. There are some areas I need to get at and the shop is out of stock."

Supervisor Jim: "No problem. I'll take care of it."

At the end of the day, Jim again swings by to acknowledge what was accomplished. He comments on how clean and organized the work station is and wishes Ken a good night. Jim lets him know he'll see him tomorrow.

By interacting three times during the day, Jim has had plenty of opportunity to observe and comment on things that are important to the company's mission. Did you recognize the following in this example?

1. The importance of a customer account (the O'Henry account).
2. Acknowledgement of a previous quality problem.
3. Awareness of Ken's workload.
4. The assignment of wiping down the keyboard and phone handset. What was that?
   a. It showed concern for all employees' health.
   b. It demonstrated good hygiene habits.
   c. It stressed the company's value of cleanliness and workplace organization.

d. It fulfilled the supervisor's role of emphasizing objectives as a part of the company's mission.
5. Recognition of Ken's productivity.
6. Taking care of a nuisance issue (out of WD-40), showing you care about little things.
7. Thanking Ken for his work and making him feel appreciated and valued.
8. Finally, in all these brief interactions Jim has made the company's expectations known, he's recognized Ken's performance, and in so doing reinforced in Ken the importance of proper workplace procedures – productivity and cleanliness – all behaviors the company wants to reinforce.

Every employee in a company deserves to know how he has done each day. The practice of **Performance Management** accomplishes that.

Major companies utilize the practice of a "three times per day walk-about". Their supervisors are taught to look at the performance in those measurable areas employees are working on and to recognize whenever there is improvement. Most companies utilizing **Performance Management** encourage their employees to chart their own progress. This ensures that employees are focusing on their objectives and know their own progress. There are no surprises with this system.

The adage, *"No news is good news"* is so very wrong. News about *improved* performance is *good news* and is worthy of recognition. **Performance Management** emphasizes:
- expectations being very clear
- daily reviews of employees' performance
- frequent recognition, frequent reward and redirection as necessary
- speaking to the behaviors you're observing
- recognizing any improvement you see
- involving your employees

- ensuring that your employees go home each day, knowing how they've done so they have real news to share with their families
- recognition from the heart

Managers cannot give insincere recognition or glad-hand an employee and expect any measure of effectiveness. Employees see right through that. A sincere *"thank you"* referencing a specific observation is very meaningful. Example: *"Joe, I saw how you waited on Mrs. Holmes. You were very professional and did a nice job. You can be sure she'll ask for you the next time she needs help. Good work!"* Performance Management must come from the heart to be effective.

Read more on recognition and redirecting behavior in Chapter 7 and on rewarding behavior in Chapter 10.

Chapter 10

Incentive Compensation

What you do is far more important than what you are paid. My hope is that you are proud of what you do, that you enjoy your work and that your job compensates you sufficiently to live reasonably well. Less than that causes stress. More than that is not necessary.

This chapter shares an approach to compensation that I've found to be one of the best methods for involving employees in the success of the business and rewarding them accordingly.

But the lessons in this chapter are not limited to the world of business employment. They can also provide effective guidelines for improving relationships in your personal life. The basic principles behind employee Incentive Compensation are equally effective when you work together with your family to complete a home project, or to save up for a new television, or to plan a family vacation.

Love,
Dad

Incentive Compensation

You've completed your strategic marketing plan. You've discovered needs that have not been met and have aligned your company to produce a product and/or service that others are not offering. Your sales are growing and your bottom line is improving.

Training has been a key for all this to happen and you are fortunate to have some great employees who have helped you develop the systems, make the products to specifications and get them delivered on time. Things are going great, as long as you can keep everyone motivated and staying with the company.

You want to address your pay systems so they motivate and keep your employees. You're now ready to implement an incentive compensation program.

The definition of motivation is *"the desire to do things."* The stronger your employees' belief is in a commonly held set of values, the greater is their desire to do things. That's why it is so important to spend time *involving* and *encouraging* your employees in all that's been shared in **Legacy**. When you do this with the heart attitude of a servant leader you will be creating in your employees a desire to do those things you want them to do.

This principle of encouragement is found in over 80 passages of scripture. Here are just a few examples:

> *"These are the things you should tell people. Encourage them, and when they are wrong, correct them."* Titus 2:15

> *"...encourage each other every day..."* Hebrews 3:13 (remember that Performance Management teaches us to have interactions with our employees three times per day)

> *"We should think about each other to see how we can encourage each other to show love and do good works."* Hebrews 10:24

Implementation: Before you begin this program with your employees, first share *why* you are doing this. Level with your employees that you believe in the principle of WIN/WIN. Share with them the concept of the Virtuous Cycle. Use this as an opportunity to share your personal values and to demonstrate those values by implementing an education program and an incentive compensation program. Share your personal belief in **servant leadership**.

As you begin your employee education program, recognize that the benefits of educating your employees to your bottom line are unquestionable. When your employees understand how the company makes money, the trust factor increases markedly. Your employees become advocates for making more money and they will find lots of ways to cut costs and increase sales.

When you close the loop by tying a portion of your employees' pay to the success of your company you will see amazing results - because your employees truly become invested in *their* company's success.

Educating your employees to the bottom line is sometimes called *open-book management*. There is an excellent book called The Great Game of Business by Jack Stack which tells the story of how sharing financial information saved a company. This book gives step-by-step instructions on how to implement this approach in your company.

Begin your incentive compensation program by teaching your employees about what makes up profit. For purposes of this example, we'll be talking about **Net Income Before Taxes (NIBT)**. Here's the formula:

Sales - returns, refunds and discounts	= Net Sales
- Costs of your product and services	= Gross Profit
- Overhead, payroll and interest on loans	= Net Income Before Taxes

What are Sales? Let's talk about what Sales really are. First of all, our emphasis can never be strictly on the top line. Why? Because the top line is never "real" nor can you spend the top line. The first place to start in your education of employees is that Net Sales are the only type of sales you'll talk about. Net Sales are what you have left over after Returns, Refunds and Discounts. The reason this is important is that it involves an area where employees have some measure of control.

What employees have control of: Improving quality is an area within employees' control that yields benefits. When employees follow your Quality Systems, there are fewer returns. Returns reduce your Net Sales so in your regular employee meetings when you review your financial performance you will want to look at every return, openly and without fear. You also will want to look at refunds that were given and why. It's also valuable to talk about discounts - why they are being offered, to whom and what the benefit of discounts are to the company (e.g., discount for payment in 10 days improves your cash flow and reduces your need to borrow). All of this is educating your employees to the bottom line.

Once you've covered what Net Sales are, show that from those sales you subtract the costs of making or providing your products and your services. Be sure to cover with your employees everything that makes up those costs. Generally speaking, your employees already have some idea of what some of these costs are, however they likely do not have a good understanding of the impact of material waste and labor waste on profits. We'll cover that in just a bit - how to explain those impacts.

Explain that **Net Sales minus Cost of Goods Sold = Gross Profit**. Gross Profit is a strategic indicator for the company because it tells you if you are in a market that will provide sufficient margins to be successful. This however is still not the data point that you will focus on. Why? Because you can't spend Gross Profit.

Now is the time for you to explain that there are certain costs that are simply a part of doing business, like it or not and these costs must be taken out of Gross Profit *before* we talk about what we really have for spendable income. Note that this example does not include the income taxes you have to pay.

Your focus should be on **Net Income Before Taxes.** Use actual, simple figures to demonstrate this to your employees. Emphasize that NIBT is what you will be talking about because it is the *only thing* that one can spend.

It's as simple as this and be careful to not make it any more complicated. Employees generally aren't interested in the fine nuances of your P&L - only the basics. Keep it easier to communicate.

How often should you communicate your P&L? Monthly, maybe more frequently in some businesses like restaurants, but at least monthly. Incentive compensation payments should coincide with this. In other words, you should pay the bonuses monthly. While monthly payments are not as large as annual bonuses, *frequent* recognition and reward is much more effective. Employees find it difficult to meaningfully connect what they do with the bonuses they receive when the frequency is longer than monthly.

The key to an effective incentive compensation program is ensuring that employees understand what they have control over - what *they* do that impacts your financial performance - so you'll want to spend a lot of time identifying those things with your employees. Let's look at the following example where you've achieved an 8% NIBT:

Educating to the Bottom Line

Sales	$ 25,000
- returns, refunds, discounts	- 500
= Net Sales	24,500
- COGS	- 10,000
= Gross Profit	14,500
- overhead, payroll, interest on loans	- 12,500
= Net Income Before Taxes (NIBT)	**$ 2,000 8% NIBT**

All graphics on pages 97-99 from
"The Principled Management Series"

The Donnachaid Group
Principled Management
Consulting

Legacy - Principled Management　　　　Incentive Compensation – 98

You'll want to do monthly "what if" scenarios:

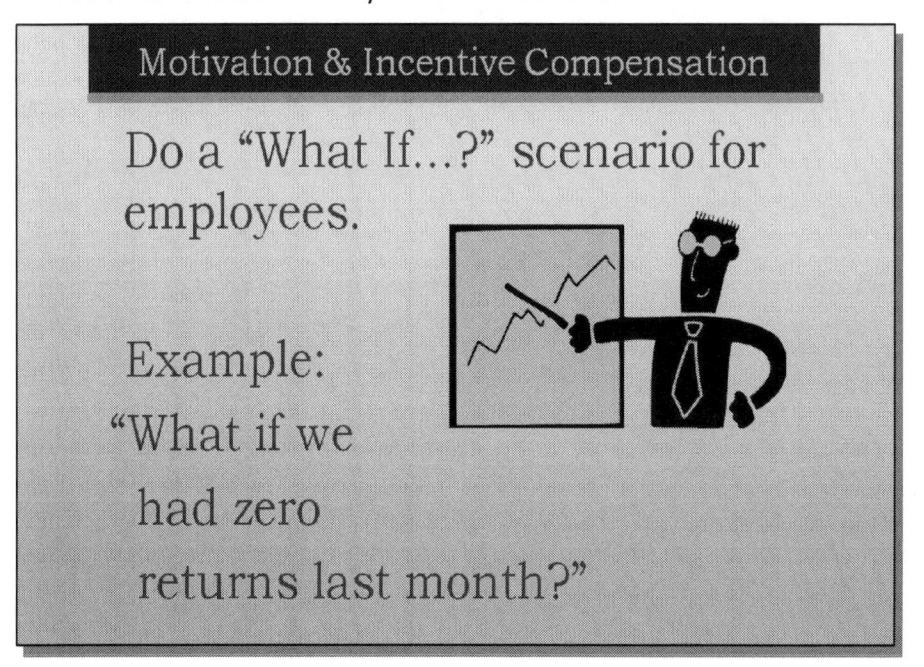

Motivation & Incentive Compensation

Do a "What If...?" scenario for employees.

Example: "What if we had zero returns last month?"

Show what zero returns does to the bottom line:

Motivation & Incentive Compensation

Sales	**$ 25,000**
- returns, refunds, discounts	- 0
= Net Sales	**25,000**
- COGS	- 10,000
= Gross Profit	**15,000**
- overhead, payroll, interest on loans	-12,500
= Net Income Before Taxes (NIBT)	**$ 2,500**　10% NIBT

Result: Net Income increases by $500, an increase from 8% to 10%...or a 25% increase in profits!

Legacy - Principled Management Incentive Compensation – 99

Now show what happens with an incentive compensation program:

Motivation & Incentive Compensation

	10% NIBT	8% NIBT
Sales	$ 25,000	$ 25,000
- returns, refunds, discounts	- 0	- 500
= Net Sales	25,000	24,500
- COGS	- 10,000	- 10,000
= Gross Profit	15,000	14,500
- overhead, payroll, interest on loans	-12,500	-12,500
= Net Income Before Taxes (NIBT)	$ 2,500	$ 2,000
Incentive Compensation bonuses		
Joe	$250	$200
Sue	$250	$200
You	$500	$400
	$ 1,000	$ 800

Your example is a company with you and two employees and a monthly payroll of $10,000 ($2500 for each of the employees and $5000 for you as owner). You've set up a simple incentive compensation program that gives monthly percentage bonuses equal to your NIBT. In our 8% example the bonus is 8% or $200 for each of your employees and $400 for you. Now show what happens with the combination of increased sales and zero returns:

Motivation & Incentive Compensation

	11.9% NIBT	10% NIBT	8% NIBT
Sales	$ 26,000	$ 25,000	$ 25,000
- returns, refunds, discounts -	0	- 0	- 500
= Net Sales	$ 26,000	25,000	24,500
- COGS	- 10,400	- 10,000	- 10,000
= Gross Profit	15,600	15,000	14,500
- overhead, payroll, interest on loans	-12,500	-12,500	-12,500
= Net Income Before Taxes (NIBT)	$ 3,100	$ 2,500	$ 2,000
Incentive Compensation bonuses			
Joe	$298	$250	$200
Sue	$298	$250	$200
You	$596	$500	$400
Total	$1192	$ 1,000	$ 800

Look at what happens when there are **no** returns and your net is 10%. Your two employees each get $250 in bonus pay and yours increases to $500 - a true WIN/WIN.

This is one simple example. But let's carry this further: what are all the cost areas that employees can impact? Quality is one we've already looked at. There's also material waste, product damage, freight costs, overtime, and on and on. You'll want to make these lists with all of your employees. But that's not the end of it. Be sure to educate your employees on how they can impact the bottom line by increasing your revenues. Everyone in your company can help impact your sales, especially in a small town market.

In this example, through the employees' efforts, sales increased $1000 in the month. By maintaining good quality and productivity, the only costs that increased were the material costs of $400. The result was a $600 improvement to the bottom line, yielding an 11.9% NIBT and an 11.9% bonus for everyone. Now, in a teaching moment you show how employees increased their bonuses by 49% (from $200 to nearly $300) by simply doing the right things and helping to bring in the additional sales. Even with the increased bonuses, your NIBT benefits - as do you.

For those of you who have an accounting interest, the way this works is that the bonuses from one month are added to the labor costs for the next month. This creates a self-balancing feature in your incentive compensation program that prevents windfalls and wild swings. A "so-so" month that follows a phenomenal month will be a little more conservative, but this too, you teach to your employees. It's all about trust and being up front with them.

Other than the individual pay information shown in these examples, you should create a simple P&L paycheck stuffer each month that has all the information you wish to share. The best way for employees to learn and the best way to earn their trust is by sharing this information with them. If you don't want your own salary to be a part of the calculations, simply modify the P&L accordingly.

Two Rules: There are basically only two rules in your incentive compensation program:

1. Every employee is eligible and involved.
2. The bonus percentage is applied to the amount of pay the employee received in the P&L month.

In your monthly employee meetings be sure to review the progress of everyone's objectives and measurements. These should be right in line with your financial performance. If they're not, you have the opportunity to do even more education on the running of a business. It all ties together and your goal is to make sure your employees see, feel and know the direct connection they have with the performance of the company and the bonus pay they are receiving. And remember to celebrate your success with your employees!

Finally, as a servant leader, you should understand that recognizing and rewarding your employees is a principle that has scriptural foundations.

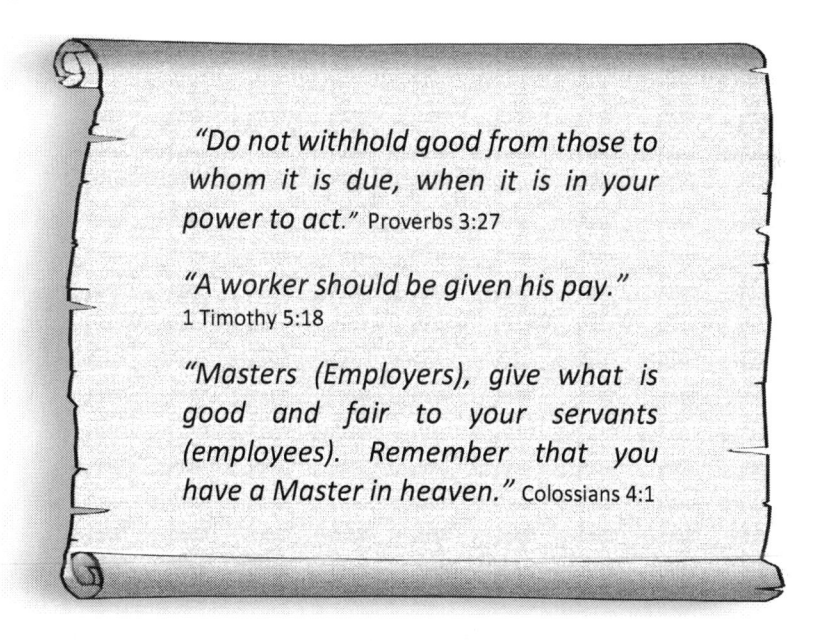

> *"Do not withhold good from those to whom it is due, when it is in your power to act."* Proverbs 3:27
>
> *"A worker should be given his pay."*
> 1 Timothy 5:18
>
> *"Masters (Employers), give what is good and fair to your servants (employees). Remember that you have a Master in heaven."* Colossians 4:1

Just two chapters left...
Nice going!

Legacy - Principled Management   Principles – 103

Chapter 11

Principles

    In previous chapters, we learned about the foundational building blocks for a business. Once the vision, values and mission have been established and the strategic planning has been completed, the essence of a business operation is in its systems. The performance of those systems and the people who own them is a continual work in progress and part of the fun of being in management.

    It's interesting, but little is said about "intuition" in business – probably because it's so difficult to define and impossible to systemize. Yet intuition is often considered one of the distinguishing characteristics that separates good leaders from great leaders.

    Why is it that some business leaders just seem to know what to do? What makes that distinguishing difference? Individual giftedness certainly plays a role, but I also believe that the assimilation of sound business principles over years of experience creates the ability to sense things and to act accordingly – even when it's not evident to others.

    This chapter documents a number of these principles for you – many with very clear scriptural underpinnings. I hope they will help you in your business and family decisions.

                                                   Love,
                                                   Dad

Principle Number 1

"Family"

I once held the position of Human Resources Manager. During those years, I developed a number of training programs. One was a Supervisors' Training Course that was held internally.

Our goal was to achieve consistency in the way supervisors addressed employee issues and to do so within the framework of the company's values. Therefore, teaching values became a prerequisite to this course.

At one of the sessions a young supervisor asked, *"Linc, why can't you just put everything into a book so we can just look up the issue and read what we're supposed to do?"* My reply was that being a manager is not that easy because there are no set rules that apply to every situation. But I did share that there is a *principle* that, if embraced, would help as a guide in most situations - the **Principle of "Family."**

The **Principle of "Family"** is not what you might imagine. It's not just the idea of treating everyone in a company like one big family, although that's certainly part of it. Rather, it relates to how we should treat each other and how we should respond to issues at work. We don't normally think about it but most of us spend more time with the people we work with than we do with our families. It's important then, that we make an effort toward having the best possible work relationships with one another.

So what is the **Principle of "Family"**? Quite simply, it's this:

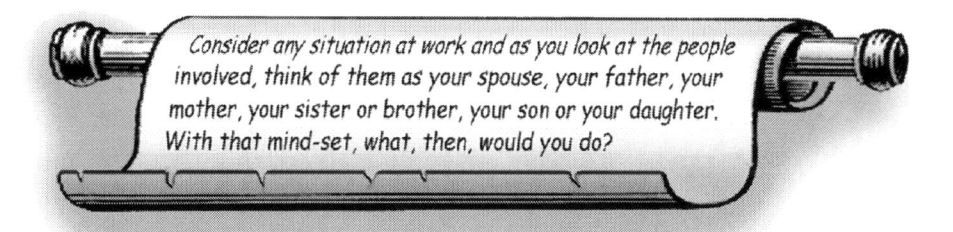

> *Consider any situation at work and as you look at the people involved, think of them as your spouse, your father, your mother, your sister or brother, your son or your daughter. With that mind-set, what, then, would you do?*

Here are a few scriptures that teach the **Principle of "Family."**

"Keep on loving one another as brothers and sisters." Hebrews 13:1

"How good and pleasant it is when God's people live together in unity!" Psalm 133:1

"...do not despise the Lord's discipline, and do not resent his rebuke, because the Lord disciplines those he loves, as a father the son he delights in." Proverbs 3:11-12

"...Love your neighbor as yourself." Matthew 22:39

"Be devoted to one another in love. Honor one another above yourselves." Romans 12:10

"Be completely humble and gentle; be patient, bearing with one another in love." Ephesians 4:2

"Therefore encourage one another and build each other up..." 1 Thessalonians 5:11

As I shared the **Principle of "Family"** with the supervisors, I challenged them to think of various situations so we could talk about the applications. Here are some examples:

<u>**Safety Training Example:**</u> You are training your mother on the operation of a punch press. You wouldn't want **anyone** to be injured on this machine - but **especially your own mother**. What do you do? You not only stress the safety protocols, you demonstrate them to your mother. You show her where the danger areas are. You ask your mother to repeat back to you what you've taught her – to

make sure she understood you. You then ask your mother to show you, step-by-step, what she learned, just to ensure that she does understand it. You provide your mother with all the necessary personal protection gear (gloves, armguards, safety glasses, hearing protection) and stress the importance of wearing this gear throughout the entire shift. The principle is this: **This is your mother**. This is *"family."* How would you feel if your mother was injured on a machine you trained her on? This is how you should feel with **anyone** you train; therefore, the **Principle of "Family"** dictates that you put the same effort into safety training with each employee as you would with your mother.

<u>Sexual Harassment Example</u>: Your daughter is working in your department. One day, as she walks to her work area, you witness Joe, a male co-worker slap her on the behind and make a crude remark to her. At this point I asked the supervisors, "How would you feel if this were your daughter?" Their responses were: "really ticked", "furious", and "madder than heck." My reply was that this is exactly how they should feel. The **Principle of "Family"** demands that.

This is your daughter. You expect her to be able to work in this company without being treated this way. Joe is clearly out of line. You should react immediately by pulling him off the production floor, taking him into your office behind closed doors, letting him know in no uncertain terms that his behavior is way off base – totally unacceptable – and that if he ever does that again, he'll be fired. Note: most firms also have specific instructions for supervisors to document and report this to their immediate supervisor and to the HR Department.

The **Principle of "Family"** does not disallow an emotional response for behavior that is so out of line. In fact it demands such a response so that all other employees see that it is clearly out of bounds to sexually harass another employee. I reinforced that supervisors should remember how they said they would feel and respond accordingly with any employee in this situation.

Tardiness Example: **Your son** was just hired in the assembly department – his first job. You are pleased to hear that he is doing good work and that he is well-liked, but you're disappointed when you see that he has been 3-7 minutes late on three separate occasions in the past two weeks. What do you do?

This is your son. You're aware that he stays up late watching television and playing video games. He has a tendency to hit the snooze button on his alarm, oversleeps and then rushes off to work without eating a decent breakfast. You know that eventually this behavior will catch up with him. Your son will likely receive a series of warnings and may lose his job. You're concerned that by the time he's 35 he will have gone through several jobs and periods of unemployment because of his lack of discipline. Again, what do you do?

As his father, the **Principle of "Family"** leads you to sit down with your son and explain the necessity of being reliable. This includes the personal discipline of eating right, sleeping right and getting up in plenty of time for work. In fact, you stress to your son that he should be at work 15 minutes before his shift starts. You give him three alarm clocks and tell him to set one next to his bed, one across the room and the third one in the bathroom – all set a few minutes apart. After a few days he will develop the discipline to get up promptly.

If this is how you would respond to your son, then it is the same way you should help out one of your employees who is having trouble getting to work on time. Treat each situation as if your family member was involved.

The supervisors explored a number of situations and in every case, treating each employee as if he was a family member gave them the guidance they needed.

As COO, I covered the **Principle of "Family"** with new employees in their orientation sessions. I found that they easily grasped this concept and appreciated that we had this principle as a corporate value.

"Interdependency"

Principle Number 2

"The combined efforts of an interdependent team will always outweigh the sum of the output of its individuals." Linc Duncanson

There's a big difference between *having supervision* and *being supervised*. Covey teaches that individuals grow through stages:

Dependence: This is when we require someone to provide for the basic necessities in life (food, shelter, and clothing). In a work setting an extreme example is when we need a supervisor to oversee what we're doing, to prod us along to keep working and to closely oversee us in order to prevent misbehavior.

Independence: This is the point at which we can fend for ourselves without the help of others. It is however, a state of "self-centeredness." You do your job. I'll do my job.

Interdependency: This is what we should all strive for because it's the state in which we not only hold our own on the job but it's when we see the value in helping others, as well as receiving help from others, to accomplish more than we could alone. In a state of interdependency a team works together in harmony with little or no supervision for the good of the company.

The **Principle of Interdependency** values the employee's level of skill and his reliability. It recognizes the trust you have in an individual's ability to work without supervision (while certainly recognizing the need for the availability of a supervisor to assist in areas outside the responsibility of the employee). This is a basic level of expectation. It means that supervisors don't have to act like the "foremen" of old. It means that supervisors are a resource to their department's employees.

The higher level of interdependency takes time and teamwork to develop and is well worth the effort. The **Principle of Interdependency** is actually a Biblical concept:

> Two are better than one, because they have a good return for their labor: if either of them falls down, one can help the other up. But pity anyone who falls and has no one to help them up. Also, if two lie down together, they will keep warm. But how can one keep warm alone? Though one may be overpowered, two can defend themselves. A cord of three strands is not easily broken. Ecclesiastes 4:9-12

It's important to remember the **Principle of Interdependency** when hiring employees. Look for those candidates who will work reliably without being supervised. Look for people who team together well and have a heart attitude to help others. Only then can you develop a high-performing interdependent team.

Principle Number 3

"Respect"

Organizations are like a living organism. They're made up of individuals, each possessing varying skills and abilities. Management's proper application of those skills in a team environment results in an output of goods and services that a company can market.

Think of all the parts in a machine. Can you afford to disregard certain parts by not giving the routine maintenance they need? Of course not. At some point your machine will fail. You must respect and value the function of each part and appreciate how all parts work together to ensure that the machine will function properly.

The same can be said for employees in a company. Every employee is worthy of your respect. And every employee needs "routine maintenance" (recognition, reward, redirection, training, etc.).

The **Principle of Respect** for one another is a key value in any organization and one that is to be reinforced daily in your interactions with employees. Biblically, the value of respecting one another is found in a number of verses:

"*Show proper respect to everyone...*" 1 Peter 2:17

"*...serve one another in love.*" Galatians 5:13

"*...in Christ we who are many form one body.*" Romans 12:5

The passage on the next page, while specifically referring to a church body, describes the need to respect all members of an organization:

"*Now the body is not made up of one part but of many. If the foot should say, 'Because I am not a hand, I do not belong to the body,' it would not for that reason stop being part of the body. And if the ear should say, 'Because I am not an eye, I do not belong to the body,' it would not for that reason stop being part of the body. If the whole body were an eye, where would the sense of hearing be? If the whole body were an ear, where would the sense of smell be? But in fact God has placed the parts in the body, every one of them, just as he wanted them to be. If they were all one part, where would the body be? As it is, there are many parts, but one body. The eye cannot say to the hand, 'I don't need you!' And the head cannot say to the feet, 'I don't need you!' On the contrary, those parts of the body that seem to be weaker are indispensable, and the parts that we think are less honorable we treat with special honor. And the parts that are unpresentable are treated with special modesty, while our presentable parts need no special treatment. But God has put the body together, giving greater honor to the parts that lacked it, so that there should be no division in the body, but that its parts should **have equal concern for each othe**r. If one part suffers, every part suffers with it; if one part is honored, every part rejoices with it.*"

1 Corinthians 12:14-27

Principle Number 4

"Don't Mess with a Person's Name or Pay"

Early in my career I heard this saying and it took awhile to sink in. The first part is really a subcategory of the **Principle of Respect**. "Don't mess with a person's name" refers to the nicknames and word games managers often ascribe to employees. Sometimes it's in rhyme, like *"Joe Schmoe, whatya know?"* Sometimes it's a play on words, like *"Gee, April, you're the employee of the month!"* (as if April has never heard that one before). In nearly all cases, it's lacking in humor at best and is derogatory at worst. A person's name is to be respected and properly used.

So what does *"Don't mess with his pay"* refer to? Quite simply, in an employee/employer relationship, it goes without saying that the employer has control over how much the employee is paid. Except in extreme cases where corrective action is being given (see Chapter 7), mentioning or joking about an employee's pay accomplishes only one thing - *it introduces fear.*

> *"Do nothing out of selfish ambition or vain conceit. Rather, in humility value others above yourself, not looking to your own interests but each of you to the interests of the others."* Philippians 2:3-4

> *"Do not take advantage of a hired worker who is poor and needy,..."* Deuteronomy 2:14

Principle Number 5

"CONTRIBUTION-BASED PAY"

"For Scripture says, 'Do not muzzle an ox while it is treading out the grain,' and 'The worker deserves his wages.'" 1 Timothy 5:18

"Do not hold back the wages of a hired worker overnight" Leviticus 19:13

I wholeheartedly believe in **Incentive Compensation Pay** as the best pay system for employees in any organization (the specifics of Incentive Compensation are covered in Chapter 10). The underlying principle is to ***pay individuals based on their contribution to the organization***. While this is the most difficult of all pay systems to create and manage, the **Principle of Contribution-Based Pay** is absolutely the fairest of all pay systems.

With a contribution-based pay system, management must determine the value of each individual's output, reviewing it frequently. Unfortunately, other than 100% commission arrangements (and even those I question) there are really no ready templates for one to use. Each pay system needs to be specifically created for each business setting. For that reason I promote the use of a labor market-based wage system (i.e., the wage range that labor surveys show for each position in the demographics of your business) to arrive at a "base range", combined with an Incentive Compensation Program that is calculated from net income performance.

One question is what to do with long term employees who have reached the top of their range. The answer varies, depending on the interest and ability of the employee to take on additional responsibilities, meriting more income. With an effective career pathing program you will have identified potential routes for employee promotions. Your role as a servant leader then, is to support the continued education and growth of those employees and promote them as the opportunities present themselves.

But what about the employee who has no desire to be promoted or lacks the potential for a leadership position? Should that person simply stagnate? Absolutely not! I contend that in any work setting management can identify areas of responsibility that can be assigned to senior employees who are at the top of their ranges. This not only creates an opportunity for additional pay (usually in the form of bonuses), it also relieves supervisors of some of the tasks they are charged with - a WIN/WIN.

If there is an age/physical capabilities issue, the **Principle of Contribution-Based Pay** leads you to assess the intellectual assets of your employee and align those with an office or lighter duty position that recognizes the years of service, the intrinsic knowledge and value this person can continue to bring to the organization. This is a situation where the **Principle of "Family"** applies. What would you do if this was your mother or father?

Principle Number 6

"Honesty"

When I was in my 20's, I went to visit my father at his workplace in the U.S. Postal Service. At that time, he was a Regional Staffing and Scheduling Officer - a fairly high position within the organization. As we were walking out of his office he stopped at a secretary's desk and asked for a postage stamp for his personal use. The secretary gave him a stamp and my father, in turn, reached in his pocket and gave her the correct change for the purchase. For some reason it impressed me that my father did this. Later in my career I applied what he had done when I needed a postage stamp. I always went to the receptionist and publicly paid for my postage. The act of the business leader paying for something as small as a stamp (or photocopies, etc.) sets the ethical tone in a company for everyone else. It demonstrates honesty and it demonstrates equality. It is the **Principle of Honesty**.

"You must have accurate and honest weights and measures, so that you may live long in the land the Lord your God is giving you. For the Lord your God detests anyone who does these things, anyone who deals dishonestly." Deuteronomy 25:15-16

"An honest answer is like a kiss on the lips." Proverbs 24:26

There is great value in owning up to mistakes. There is credibility in admitting your faults. Honesty in all things at all levels is an "absolute" principle. Don't even allow joking about "a second set of books" or "an underhanded deal." There is no place for that in any ethical business. The **Principle of Honesty** is the best and the *only* policy and is a principle to live by.

Principle Number 7

"CONFRONTATION"

In an interdependent work environment management supports the self-policing of values. To do that, the value of confronting one another when values are being violated needs to be taught. Why? Because there is a right way and a wrong way to confront a person. The **Principle of Confrontation** requires that:

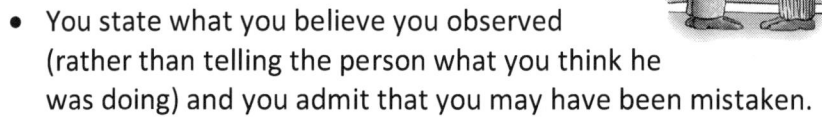

- You state what you believe you observed (rather than telling the person what you think he was doing) and you admit that you may have been mistaken.
- You state that you believe it is important to guard our values.
- You state the company value that you feel was violated.
- You allow the person to share his side of the story.
- If there is an admission and apology, you accept it and move on.
- If there is a denial that the violation occurred, you accept it and move on.
- If there is a disagreement about something actually being a value, you suggest that the two of you meet with your manager to clarify the value.

"...go and point out their fault, just between the two of you." Matthew 18:15

"...restore that person gently." Galatians 6:1

With this respectful approach, you will build relationships and reinforce values. In some cases the result may be that an employee leaves but if the violator doesn't subscribe to the values of the company, then he shouldn't be working there anyway.

Managers have an obligation to confront employees when there is a violation of values but the best scenario is when employees feel comfortable enough with each other to do this peer-to-peer. It's worth striving for.

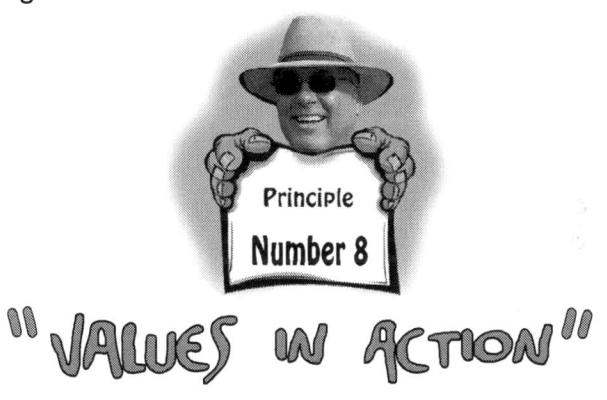

Principle Number 8
"Values in Action"

So often in business you will be presented with a situation where the application of your values comes into play. For example, when a manager reports a billing error where a customer has been overcharged, use the occasion as an opportunity to demonstrate the company's "values in action" by commenting, *"Well, of course, honesty is the only policy."*

As a servant leader, your emphasis is on how we act. You remind others of the "guideposts" that keep the company on the straight and narrow. The more opportunities you have to demonstrate the company's values, the sooner they will become engrained in the corporate culture.

When there is a significant demonstration of **The Principle of "Values in Action"** - like the story of the department employees who did the work of an injured co-worker so she could continue being paid - you should share that story in employee meetings and orientations.

Remember... your credibility and reputation are formed from what you *do*, not what you say.

Principle Number 9

"Owning Problems"

You can hide problems and pretend they're not there or you can own your problems and demonstrate both your values and your skills to solve them. The **Principle of Owning Problems** requires honesty about what has happened and why. It utilizes any number of problem-solving disciplines and it brings others in as resources, recognizing their talents and the need for interdependency. It avoids finger-pointing.

We're all human. We all make mistakes. And sometimes despite our best efforts, we're faced with unforeseen problems. Own the problem. Analyze the problem. State the issue and reveal the data behind the issue. Admit that you could have done things differently and learn from the experience. Make ownership of problems a "value" in your organization.

Principle Number 10

"Quality vs. PRODUCTIVITY"

I have to admit that early in my own career, I would get irritated when we would be discussing productivity at an employee meeting and someone would challenge, *"Well, what do you want - quality or quantity?"* I probably irritated some of the employees when I would quickly respond, *"Both!"*

In time, I learned that it is necessary to establish some priorities between quality and productivity. **The Principle of Quality vs. Productivity** sets the record straight. How? By looking at what your *customer* deems to have value.

The saying, *"Good, Fast or Cheap – Pick Two"* points out the supposed conflicts in producing a product or providing a service. But think about it. When you make an important purchase there is one requirement that is always at the top - quality. I do not hold that **Quality vs. Productivity** is an "either/or" decision. You can and should achieve both. I do believe, however, that quality always trumps productivity. Why? Because quality is what the customer deems to have *value* and therefore, is willing to pay for. Let me explain:

Will your customer pay for a quality product he is purchasing? Yes, by all means. Will your customer pay for a fancy chair you just purchased for your office? No way! Your customer doesn't care what kind of chair you sit in - and certainly isn't going to pay for it. Similarly, your customer does not wish to "pay" for your lack of productivity, your scrap, your need to use overtime (in most cases), your safety or your cleanliness. Now as a manager, all of these things are important to you, but you can only charge your customers for what they ascribe *value* to.

For that reason, your Quality Policy needs to have built-in priorities that are very clear to employees.

1. The Quality of our products and services is our highest priority (the customer pays for this).

2. The promised On-Time Delivery of our products and services is our next priority (the customer pays for this).

3. Productivity and making a profit on our products and services is our third priority (the customer does not care about this - but you do).

4. Working safely is an "overriding priority" (the customer does not care about this – but you do).

5. Working in a clean and organized environment is our next priority (the customer does not care about this – but you do).

Now when I state "the customer does not care," I don't mean that the customer is callous to what happens to your company but the reality is, the customer cannot afford to "care" in the sense of paying for your issues. The customer does not know whether you had scrap problems, overruns, or that someone was injured on the job. Your customer *should not* know about these issues. They are *your* issues - not your customer's.

Regarding productivity, the best approach is to first teach quality, then teach methods and systems that help employees improve their productivity. Reducing or eliminating mistakes will have a marked impact on an employee's productivity and morale. Soon it will be evident that the employee can achieve a high level of quality at an improved rate of productivity. For more on this, read the section on Performance Management.

Regarding safety, the term "overriding priority" means this: Safety is something that is in everything you do - it's not a separate category. In producing a quality product and delivering on time, it is expected that employees are working in a safe environment, using safe methods. But safety cannot be declared the number one priority for a business. No one starts up a business just to be safe. No, the existence of the business and its offering to the marketplace is the number one priority. If ever there is a safety concern, then safety automatically takes the overriding position. You never proceed in an unsafe scenario.

Teach your Quality Policy to your employees. **The Principle of Quality vs. Productivity** directs you to do this in a way that is simple, and that captures key words such as:

> *"We deliver quality products on time, profitably,*
> *in a clean and safe workplace."*

You would be hard-pressed to find a more succinctly stated quality policy. It sets forth all the measurables necessary for successful Performance Management: quality, on time delivery, profitability, safety and cleanliness.

> **"...their work will be shown for what it is."**
> 1 Corinthians 3:13

Legacy - Principled Management   Principles – 122

Principle Number 11

"Cutting Problems in Half"

This is a simple principle. When facing large, complex issues, your team can sometimes get overwhelmed. The **Principle of Cutting Problems in Half** is just what it states: Break your problem into manageable chunks beginning with that which must be completed first. Assign measurable tasks and spread out the assignments (divide and conquer). Continue to do this until you've resolved the issue.

The building of the Panama Canal must have seemed like an impossible task to most but it began with one shovel and a single scoop of dirt.

Principle Number 12

Don't Sink the Ship

This is a principle that puts things in perspective and allows for innovation without fear of failure. The **Don't Sink the Ship Principle** comes into play when your management team is concerned about the financial impact of a failed project - so they do nothing. Your message should be this:

"While trying to succeed, everyone should be permitted to experience some failures, up to $____. But that also requires your department's systems to be robust enough to prevent a major catastrophe that would 'sink the ship'."

Everyone has the right and obligation to explore and innovate. Notice however, that you must set the parameters on the maximum amount that can be risked in these ventures. Parameters generally vary by department function and level of management. No one has the right, however, to do anything that would adversely affect the livelihood of everyone else in the company. In other words, no one can do something that would "sink the ship."

The **Don't Sink the Ship Principle** is a good one to share in employee meetings when reviewing the root cause of quality issues. Failure to do a quality check on one component can potentially result in a major product recall which could become a "sink the ship" issue. Managers and employees need to understand this principle.

"ON TIME DELIVERY: THE SPIKE PRINCIPLE"

Principle Number 13

Most companies have one or more "premier customers" who get top attention and priority as needed. Typically, these are higher volume customers and despite the best planning and systems, you will occasionally face a demand for an order that completely wipes out your capacity and/or your materials. This is not so affectionately called a "spike."

Normally, the importance of this large customer has been so engrained in the company with phrases like, *"Anything they want... They're top dog... They always come first,"* etc., that employees naturally feel that they must turn the entire operation over to meeting this premier customer's needs, regardless of the impact on other lesser customers.

The problem is, you have many other customers who also rely on your capacity and materials to make their products and those orders are now going to be late. While you'll meet the requirements of the one customer, you will now face far too many late orders with the rest of your customers. Most in your company will feel this is unavoidable. They're wrong.

This **Spike Principle** directs us to do just the opposite of the prevailing thinking in your company. You should first carve out all the orders that would be impacted by the spike and schedule them to be completed right away. You then calculate from your remaining capacity and materials how much of your premier customer's order you can complete and when the balance will be completed. You address this with your customer (who, by the way, is very aware of the spike they've created) and you negotiate a workable solution with them.

Would your premier customer allow you to cause multiple late orders with other accounts? Probably. Remember that this is not something they can afford to "care" about. But would your premier customer hold it against you for not being able to produce the entire order at one time? Probably not, particularly since they know what you are capable of doing and let's face it - they also experience spikes.

The **Spike Principle** eliminates unnecessary chaos and costs. Make sure your management knows this principle.

Principle Number 14 — "Pace"

Think of an organization as a living, breathing organism with many parts. While each part has a different function, all parts need to work together to ensure a smooth operation.

The Principle of Pace recognizes the importance of all the parts of an organization moving along in synch without one department getting out too far ahead of the rest or another department lagging too far behind the others.

A good visual for you to consider is that of a large army moving along a front. As the general, imagine that you are standing on a hillside looking down at all the units. To ensure a successful military campaign your responsibility is to see that all your units move along at the same pace so there are no breaches.

A leader must always have a good vantage point. If you are not on the hillside, you won't be able to see this big picture. Remember this, because while the leader must stay close to his people, at the same time he must view the organization from afar to gain the proper perspective.

The Principle of Pace requires you to shore up those who are lagging and to hold back those who are getting too far ahead. An example of this is when a sales team learns of a new product soon to be launched. Excited, they go out and begin selling the product before it's been thoroughly tested and ready for market. The sales team must be slowed down. Another example is of a marketing team who has the assignment to create the packaging design for a new line of products, but unfortunately hasn't gotten the proofs back from the marketing agency. The company risks missing its product launch just before the holidays, a prime buying time. This department needs additional resources and leadership to catch up with the rest of the organization.

A good servant leader will learn the **Principle of Pace** early in his career.

> *"...everything should be done in a fitting and orderly way."*
> I Corinthians 14:40

Principle Number 15 "Joseph"

I love the **Joseph Principle**. Remember the story of Joseph in Genesis? Through a series of events Joseph was sold into slavery by his brothers and ended up in an Egyptian prison, but after interpreting Pharaoh's dream, Joseph was put in charge of running the entire nation.

Having experienced the bumper crop of grain that God had promised for seven consecutive years, Joseph set a plan in motion for storing reserves for the next seven years of severe famine that God had also promised. When the drought began, Egypt was in the enviable position of having more than enough grain to feed its own citizens and was able to sell its excess grain to neighboring countries, greatly increasing Egypt's wealth.

Joseph's Principle of being frugal during good times allowed him to leverage his inventory and capitalize on the market conditions (the famine) when it hit. Businesses normally have cycles of ups and downs and business leaders need to understand the importance of the **Joseph Principle** to position their companies to weather the sparse times. This is not just a bottom line principle. The **Joseph Principle** applies to your decision to keep employees working during lean times. Proper management and foresight makes this possible.

There are many other lessons to learn from the story of Joseph, including what your attitude should be during times of duress. I encourage you to read chapters 37-50 in Genesis.

Principle Number 16

"Sweating the Small Stuff"

You've often heard *"Don't sweat the small stuff,"* but I think that's poor advice. Here's why.

In any organization, its systems should repeatedly and consistently produce the products or services they were designed to offer. Little flaws and errors, while seemingly insignificant, are really important indicators to you that something is wrong with the system. These act as early warning devices, allowing you to dig into the system to see what's happening.

The **Principle of "Sweating the Small Stuff"** will have you looking into things that most managers just let pass. This is not nitpicking. This is systems analysis. For example, the presence of a few drops of oil under a machine may be the sign of something much larger, if not attended to.

> *"For want of a nail the shoe was lost.*
> *For want of a shoe the horse was lost.*
> *For want of a horse the rider was lost.*
> *For want of a rider the message was lost.*
> *For want of a message the battle was lost.*
> *For want of a battle the kingdom was lost.*
> *And all for the want of a horseshoe nail."*
>
> Early proverb, author unknown

Sweat the small stuff. You'll be glad you did.

Principle Number 17

"Knowing When You're in Trouble"

Companies should not be run by fear. Deming points out that fear is destructive and kills productivity. In an organization where trust and respect are key values there should be an absence of fear.

That being said, there are boundaries in a company based on job responsibility and authority levels. Even when employees have the best intentions, they need to know what these boundaries are to prevent major mishaps. They need to know the consequences of crossing these boundaries. In other words, *people need to know when they'll be in trouble*.

The Principle of Knowing When You're in Trouble simply states that parameters for critical business systems need to be clearly in place, clearly communicated to employees as to what they are and why they are important and along with these explanations, the consequences of overstepping these boundaries need to be clearly stated and enforced.

On a trip to Disney World, everyone was wowed by a staged tsunami which knocked a semi-truck off a hill, gushing water everywhere. On the tram to the next attraction we got to see the back side of the tsunami site where I noticed a large control panel that had this signage:

⚠ **WARNING**
Anyone who opens this panel will be fired!

Now I'm not sure what issues Disney World had with this control panel but the message to employees was very clear.

The Principle of Knowing When You're in Trouble came into play with scrap control. Having done a fairly good job of eliminating major mistakes, our accumulative scrap nevertheless continued to grow. In analyzing this we discovered that the problem consisted of an accumulation of many small scrap amounts on nearly every job by nearly every employee on every shift. It was only a few dollars here and there - nothing that came to anyone's attention - but when added up, it amounted to substantial waste over the course of a year.

After a closer look, we discovered that while there were posted standards there was very little oversight of these daily performance concerns (they were so small) and therefore, there were no consequences for them either. We realized that we had to change the entire mindset of the workforce. How did we do that?

1. First of all, we openly owned the problem (see the **Principle of Owning Problems**). Not surprisingly, there were many who didn't see it as a problem.
2. We then explained the impact of the problem on our financial performance. Even after doing this, we still experienced resistance.
3. We shared what had to be done by every employee on every job on every shift to address this problem. The resistance was even greater when we did this since this required a change in the way things were being done.
4. We created three levels of authority for decision-making on production runs:
   a. Operator level
   b. Supervisor or Engineer Level
   c. Upper Management Level
5. We created visuals and charts denoting when to stop (standards were still posted, but these visuals required operators to actually stop the operation). We discovered that many times the intent was to make sure the customer got his

order on time (a good intent) but operators didn't realize the financial impact of continuing the run. These visuals included mini-stop signs in some cases.

6. We stated that no one would be in trouble for stopping a run but anyone who went beyond the stop signs – beyond his level of authority – risked losing his position in the company. He would be in trouble.

Was this introducing fear into the organization? Perhaps in one sense, but only to those who were not following what were now very clear parameters with stated consequences. We handled this as follows:

1. We reinforced that no one in the company had the right to jeopardize the livelihood of the rest of the employees by failing to follow instructions.

2. We passed on a portion of the savings in scrap to every employee in the form of monthly incentive compensation bonuses.

3. In subsequent months we shared in each meeting how the employees' efforts to reduce these small amounts of scrap added up to sizeable improvements to our bottom line and therefore, sizeable increases in their bonuses!

At first glance, the **Principle of Knowing When You're in Trouble** sounds like old school management but applied as explained above it really gives freedom to the organization. People need to know what their boundaries are in order for them to work at peak performance levels. People need certainty in their work environments so they're not second-guessing decisions. And finally, management needs strict adherence to critical business systems policies – to prevent a "Sink the Ship" scenario – without the need for long lists of "dos" and "don'ts." Finally, the **Principle of Knowing When You're in Trouble** should only be applied to the critical business systems in your company.

Legacy - Principled Management   Principles – 132

Principle Number 18

"Say it Once, Say it Twice..."

"When you have something you want people to know, say it once, say it twice, say it over and over again until you think that everyone is sick and tired of hearing it - and then say it one more time!"

Floyd Johnson, Currier Manufacturing Company, Inc.

This principle is an old marketing adage and relates to the Rule of 17 (how many times the market needs to see your ads before it really sinks in, specifically referring to market presence). It is so relevant to employee communications, particularly to your efforts to engrain your vision, mission, values and quality policy in your employees' thinking.

Repetition is the key. Good business leaders learn to *"say it once, say it twice...."*

Principle Number 19

"The 30 Second Elevator Summary"

It's recognized that every salesperson needs a 30 second "elevator" summary. What do I mean by that?

This comes from the experience of an outside salesperson who is waiting for an elevator and totally without notice, comes face to face with Mr. Jones, the president of a potential customer who is riding on the elevator with him. He now has a rare opportunity. He introduces himself to Mr. Jones who replies, *"Tell me about your company."* This is the opportunity every salesperson dreams about and this is when every salesperson needs **the 30 Second Elevator Summary**. Here's an example of how he might have replied:

> *"I am glad to tell you about our company, Mr. Jones. Since 1915, Currier Manufacturing has been manufacturing a line of over 200 steel office accessories sold direct to over 2000 retail stationers. Our claim to fame is that we ship all orders in 48 hours complete, with no back orders - and we are very interested in serving you."*

The 30 Second Elevator Summary works for all sorts of occasions: tradeshows, golf outings, running into old acquaintances (it's sometimes referred to as a curbside summary), family and friends. Be sure to create your **30 Second Elevator Summary.**

Principle Number 20

"The Moose Dance"

The Moose Dance Principle is attributed to my dear friend and mentor, Jim Hoopes, who helped me greatly as I took on the role of Sales Manager. A seasoned sales veteran, Jim shared with me what the early stages of a sales negotiation were like - when companies were just getting to know each other.

"Do you know about the Moose Dance?" Jim asked. I did not.

"Well, have you ever seen moose going through their mating ritual?" I confessed that I had not witnessed that event. Jim went on to explain. "The moose face each other. They move one way and then the other, all the time checking each other out - back and forth - like a dance. And eventually they come together. That's the Moose Dance!"

Jim went on to share how in the early developmental stages of a customer relationship it's important to "under-promise" and "over-perform." This is your opportunity to make a good first impression with a customer. This is **The Moose Dance Principle.**

Principle Number 21

"Dance with the One You Brought to the Dance"

As long as we're talking about dancing, this is a simple yet frequently violated customer service principle that I'd like to share. When you are involved with a customer, *that customer* is your most important customer and deserving of all your attention. That's why I am not a big fan of company events where multiple customers are invited.

Have you ever been to a store and as the clerk is waiting on you, he takes a phone call and waits on the caller instead of you? How did that make you feel? You've just been dumped! The person on the phone apparently is more important than you.

As absurd as this sounds, it happens all the time in retail business and store clerks act as if there's nothing wrong with this. It's like taking your date to a dance and then dumping her and dancing with someone else instead. **The "Dance with the One You Brought to the Dance" Principle** reminds us of the importance of a one-on-one relationship with each customer. Good business leaders ensure that this is engrained in the company's sales training, practices and systems.

Principle Number 22

"Contracting Up Front"

My friend Bill Hannon of Compass Consulting often shares a quote from his favorite consulting guru, Peter Block, author of Flawless Consulting: *"When consultants talk about their disasters, their conclusion is usually that the project was faulty in the initial contracting stage."* Consulting relationships are heavily weighted on trust. The company's expectations of the outcomes from the consulting project therefore, need to be clearly stated, as do the consultant's expectations of the company's commitment to the project. This is the best way to avoid misunderstandings and dissatisfaction.

The Principle of Contracting Up Front goes beyond the field of consulting. It can be applied in any job hire or promotion. It can be applied as a prelude to major task assignments. It also should be a part of your Performance Management practices. Even in areas where exact measurements are difficult (e.g., coaching), one can always state what "success" would be and can measure against that statement.

In your personal family life, **the Principle of Contracting Up Front** is a valuable parenting tool. It reinforces planning, commitment, recognition and reward. Clearly state what you expect and ensure that a commitment is voiced in return.

As a business leader, recognize when it's important to contract up front, not solely as a negotiation tool but as the use of a principle that ensures both parties will be satisfied with the results. It should be one of your values in business and life.

Principle Number 23

"FINANCIAL COLLECTIONS"

I first learned this strategic principle at an American Management Association financial seminar designed for business leaders and I learned the collection tactic from one of my mentors, Floyd Johnson. **The Financial Principle of Collections** states that you first identify the top 10% of your best paying customers. Then you identify the bottom 10% of your worst paying customers. Your strategy is this:

- If ever there is an issue with the late payment of a bill involving one of your top 10% best paying customers *you always assume that you are the one at fault* and that is the attitude you display when communicating with your customer.

- For the 10% worst paying customers you create a specific control strategy for each account, noting what the sales group can and cannot do and managing the risk, account by account, including dropping the customer if necessary.

Banks are notorious for treating all of their customers the same, regardless of their financial history. Their policies are protectionist in nature and tend to offend their good customers. As a business leader, you cannot afford to allow this to happen. By separating the top and bottom 10% of your customers, you will be able to set up separate recognition systems throughout your entire organization to ensure an appropriate response when serving your customers.

I'm afraid you misunderstood our ad... when we referred to our "Low Interest Loans," we meant we have very little interest in making the loan you're asking for!

Ben Scrooge
Loan Officer

I learned the following collection tactic (for customers not in the top 10% of best payers):

> "Hello, Mr. Smith. This is John Jessup from ABC Company. I'm calling about your invoice #254 dated April 7th for $1000. Our records show that this invoice is 20 days overdue. As you know, our terms are a strict net 30 days." [and then be silent]

Allow the customer to then make whatever statements he wishes to share and, unless he is claiming some type of mistake on your part (for which you would respond that you will immediately check it out and get back to him), simply wait in silence until the customer makes you a promise – any promise – which you can respond to.

If the promise the customer makes (e.g. *"I'll get you your $1000 by June 15")* is reasonable, then reply as follows:

> *"June 15th? That would be very much appreciated. I'll look for your check on the 15th. Thank you, Mr. Smith. We appreciate your business."*

Immediately following this conversation Mr. Jessup takes a copy of the invoice and writes a personal note in red ink on the invoice: *"Mr. Smith, Thank you for your payment by June 15th. John Jessup."* He then mails this to Mr. Smith's personal attention and logs in his timekeeper a tickler reminder for June 15th to see if the check arrived.

If the check did not arrive on June 15th, here's the scenario:

> *"Hello, Mr. Smith. This is John Jessup from ABC Company. I'm calling about your invoice #254 dated April 7th for $1000 that is now 39 days overdue. When we last spoke, you promised payment by today."* [and then be silent]

This is the point when Mr. Smith needs to be faced with his broken promise to you but it's done in absolute silence. When I first witnessed this practice I was amazed at the impact of that silence. It's much worse than yelling. My experience has been that the customer's next commitment generally yields payment. If not, then you have other decisions to make, including "red listing" this account.

The key to this practice is to make it personal. Note that Mr. Jessup said *"I'll look for your check..."* not *"We'll look for your check..."* Notice also that the memo to the customer is personally written and signed by Mr. Jessup. If your customer has an ounce of decency, this approach of playing on his ethics and personal commitment is very effective.

The Financial Principle of Collections has an added benefit. It ensures that you will not offend one of your best paying customers.

Principle Number 24

"Wiggle Room"

Ok, this is a layman's adaptation of Process Capability Critical (Cpk), the statistical measurement of any system or process and its ability to produce an output within specification limits. The study of Six Sigma systems is important for all business leaders.

The Wiggle Room Principle simply recognizes that there is variation in any system and that managers need to understand what that variation is and take steps to reduce it and center the process. After all that, managers must resist the temptation to promise better than what is statistically possible.

Particularly for custom service or product applications where there are unknowns, **the Wiggle Room Principle** reminds you to set parameters that are *easily* achievable and meet your customer's needs.

In cases where customers ask for specifications that are beyond the capabilities of your equipment, materials, staffing skills, etc., it is important that your sales staff is honest about the potential outcome and not be talked into something that you cannot perform, even if this means walking away from the opportunity.

Give yourself some wiggle room. Make sure that you can more than meet your customer's expectations.

Principle Number 25

"Trial Basis"

The Trial Basis Principle is similar to the **Wiggle Room Principle.** It recognizes that new processes need to be tested before you can declare capability and commitment. The **Trial Basis Principle** is much broader in scope and applies to products, service programs, employee policies, systems implementation and marketing. It is particularly important when considering changes to very sensitive wage and benefit areas like bonus programs or health insurance.

Why do things on a **Trial Basis**? Because human nature is to call any new initiative that does not produce the expected results a *failure.* Most employees have great difficulty in creating a new product or launching a new market offering only to see it fizzle out. It's a mindset that business leaders need to be sensitive to.

Your approach should be to present these initiatives as something you want the company to *try and assess* - that it might not work out - but even if that's the case, people are to learn from it and try something else. You don't want employees to get too emotionally attached to the initiative until it's really proven itself and then you will want to document the process and follow your business systems to ensure its repeatability and reliability.

The Trial Basis Principle takes the heat off from those involved in the experiment (and yes, be sure to call it an *experiment* or a *trial*). It allows you to recognize people for their efforts regardless of the success or failure of the initiative. It promotes innovation without fear. It's a principle business leaders need to embrace.

Principle Number 26

"Labor as a Fixed Asset"

Why do some business owners get all excited about new machines they've purchased yet neglect the value of experienced employees in their companies? Why do some business owners treat their machines better than their employees?

Well obviously, these business leaders simply don't get it. In their financial statements they show the value of their equipment under "fixed assets" and while there is no place for them to enter "employees", why wouldn't they consider them as valuable fixed assets?

The Principle of Labor as a Fixed Asset is closely tied to the value of **Employees for Life**. You've invested in your employees, providing training and expertise, building interdependent teams, developing distinctive competencies and benefiting from their years of experience. Can you afford *not* to treat them as highly valuable?

When a business owner truly adopts the **Principle of Labor as a Fixed Asset**, it is reflected in the company's policies, communications and commitment to the well-being of its employees. Combined with the **Principle of Family,** a company's values will be clearly evident and employees will recognize and appreciate this in turn.

"Masters (Employers)*, provide your slaves* (employees) *with what is right and fair, because you know that you also have a Master in heaven."* Colossians 4:1

Principle Number 27

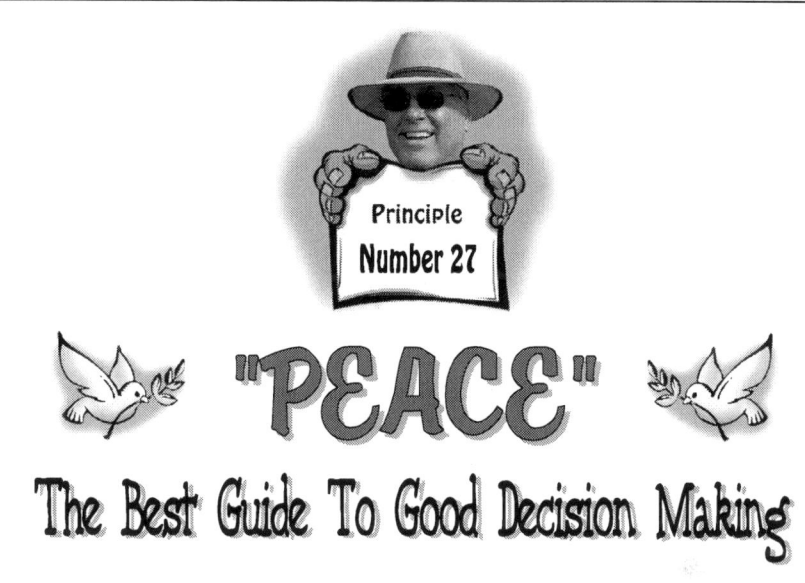

"PEACE"
The Best Guide To Good Decision Making

Buyer's remorse is an interesting description of someone who made a decision and then regretted it later. In business there are always going to be difficult decisions to make. If you've applied the **Principle of Family** and are still in doubt about what to do, my first suggestion is to wait.

Rushing into a decision when you are uncertain is generally unwise. Yet, doing nothing - a "non-choice" – can also be a bad decision. My good friend Bruce Torell, an experienced business leader, once counseled me as I was facing a difficult decision. He said, *"Linc, if you do nothing, what's the worst that will happen and how will you feel about that?"* This was very helpful advice as it put into perspective the consequences of not doing anything.

When you are ill at ease about making a decision, that's a signal you should heed. Your mind and body reacts to this uneasiness – some call it a "gut reaction" – and it's generally a signal to stop and think about what you're doing. It's also an indicator that you might need the counsel of other trusted business associates.

There were many times in my career when I was not sure of the best decision to make. Managers learn that you can't always have all the information you want yet you can't wait too long or you may lose the opportunity or the situation might even worsen. At times like these I learned to stop, put the matter to prayer, ask the Lord for direction and sleep on it. I committed that I would not act until I was at peace about the matter. This is the **Principle of Peace** and it greatly lessens the weight of your decision in that you are turning the matter over to the Lord for guidance. If when I woke up I was at peace about the matter, I would make the decision. If however I was not at peace, I would not move ahead and would seek outside advice and consider alternatives.

The Principle of Peace is more than just a "feel good" process. It's a matter of faith. It is, I believe, one of the strong suits of the Christian walk. It's not an "I" thing. It's being sensitive to the Spirit's leading, combined with using the talents God has given you.

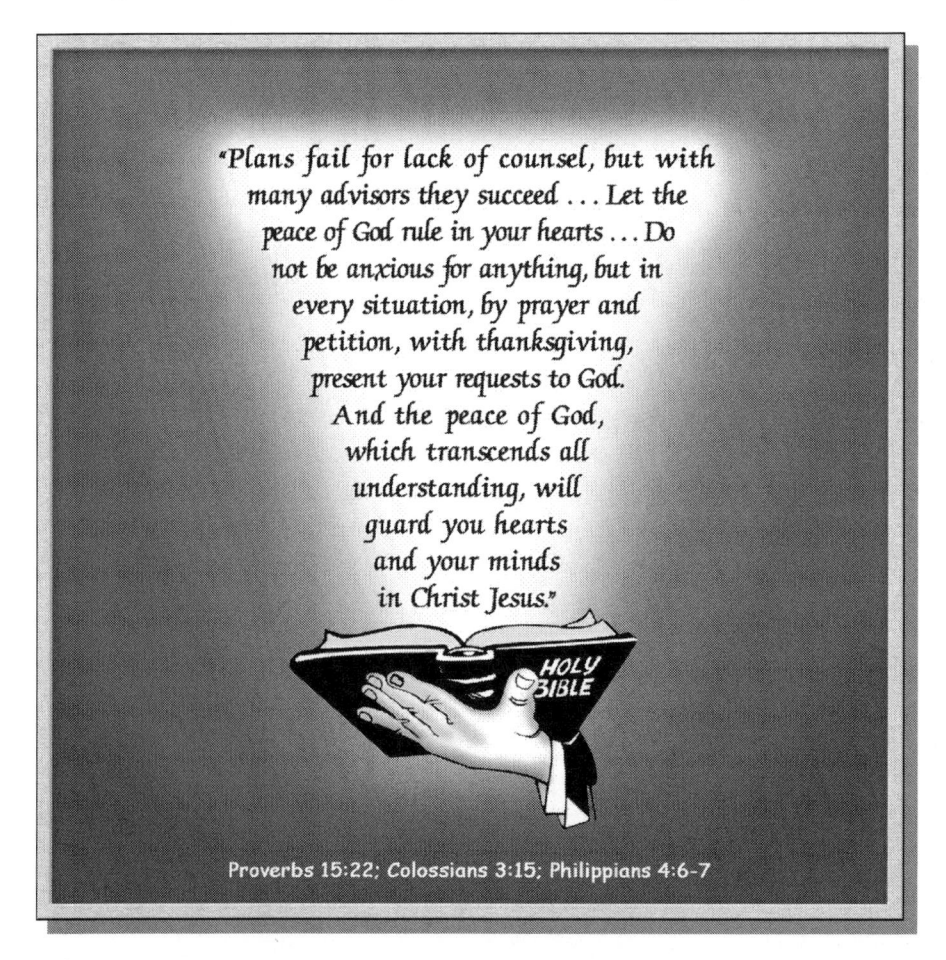

> "Plans fail for lack of counsel, but with many advisors they succeed ... Let the peace of God rule in your hearts ... Do not be anxious for anything, but in every situation, by prayer and petition, with thanksgiving, present your requests to God. And the peace of God, which transcends all understanding, will guard you hearts and your minds in Christ Jesus."
>
> Proverbs 15:22; Colossians 3:15; Philippians 4:6-7

Chapter 12
When It's All Said and Done

Who judges your performance? Who are you really working for? How will you feel about your efforts at the end of your career? What do you want people to say about you when your life is over?

These are all questions to which you will hopefully find answers while you are young.

At the end of time, of course, there is only one Judge, the Lord Jesus Christ. Whatever you do in life, finish well.

Love,
Dad

When It's All Said and Done

Robert Greenleaf, the founder of the modern Servant Leadership movement wrote:

"The servant-leader is servant first . . .

(this) begins with the natural feeling that one wants to serve. That person is sharply different from one who is leader first, perhaps to assuage an unusual power drive or acquire material possessions."

The best test, he goes on to say, is whether...

"...those served grow as persons, become healthier, wiser, freer, more autonomous, more likely themselves to become servants."

Our Lord's example as a servant-leader was one of love for others, unselfishness and personal sacrifice. He didn't use threats or fear tactics nor did he wield his authority as the earthly rulers did. Look how his disciples grew into servant-leaders themselves and impacted the whole world!

We can each become servant-leaders at work, at home and in our churches. Mothers and fathers have daily opportunities to demonstrate servant leadership with their children. Employers not only have this opportunity but also have an obligation, for...

"Whatever you do, work at it with all your heart, as working for the Lord, not for men, since you know that you will receive an inheritance from the Lord as a reward. It is the Lord Christ you are serving." Colossians 3:23-24

Embracing the heart attitude of a servant-leader puts a whole new perspective on what you do. The Bible has much to say about Christian leadership. The 2nd chapter of Proverbs instructs us to first seek wisdom and to walk with integrity:

"Tune your ears to wisdom, and concentrate on understanding. Cry out for insight, and ask for understanding. Search for them as you would for silver; seek them like hidden treasures. Then you will understand what it means to fear the LORD, and you will gain knowledge of God. For the LORD grants wisdom! From his mouth come knowledge and understanding. He grants a treasure of common sense to the honest. He is a shield to those who walk with integrity. He guards the paths of the just and protects those who are faithful to him. Then you will understand what is right, just, and fair, and you will find the right way to go." Proverbs 2:2-9

> It was Jesus himself who specifically established the model of servant leadership when he gathered his disciples together and said,

"You know that the rulers in this world lord it over their people, and officials flaunt their authority over those under them. But among you it will be different. Whoever wants to be a leader among you must be your servant, and whoever wants to be first among you must become your slave. For even the Son of Man came not to be served but to serve others and to give his life as a ransom for many." Matthew 20: 25-28 (New Living Translation)

> The Apostle Paul may have had Jesus' teaching in mind when he wrote,

"No one should seek their own good,
but the good of others."
1 Corinthians 10:24

No matter what your leadership role in life is, when you are committed to serving the Lord first, then others, you will be able to look back on your life - *your legacy* - and say . . .

"I have fought the good fight, I have finished the race, I have kept the faith."

2 Timothy 4:2

Love,
Dad

Recommended Reading & Other Resources

Applied Strategic Planning: How to Develop a Plan That Really Works
   Leonard Goodstein

A Small Business is Not a Little Big Business
   John A. Welsh and Jerry F. White

Blue Ocean Strategy
   W. Chan Kim and Renee Mauborgne

Built to Last: Successful Habits of Visionary Companies
   Jim Collins

Business by the Book
   Larry Burkett

Competing on the Eight Dimensions of Quality
   David A. Garvin

Decoding the DNA of the Toyota Production System
   Steven Spear and H. Kent Bowen

Double-Digit Growth
   Michael Treacy

Execution: The Discipline of Getting Things Done
   Larry Bossidy

Future Careers: The High-Potential Jobs of Tomorrow
   Richard W. Samson

Good to Great: Why Some Companies Make the Leap...and Others Don't
   Jim Collins

Handbook to Leadership: Leadership in the Image of God
   Ken Boa

How to Segment Industrial Markets
   Benson P. Shapiro and Thomas V. Bonoma

Leadership That Gets Results
   Daniel Goleman

Making It In America: Proven Paths to Success from 50 Top Companies
   Jerry Jasinowski

Marketing Models
   Articles by Micheal Treacy & Fred Wiersema

Marketing As Strategy: Understanding the CEO's Agenda for Driving Growth and Innovation   Nirmalya Kumar

Mind Over Technology
   Richard W. Samson

Legacy

On Becoming A Servant Leader
  Robert K. Greenleaf

Organizational Vision for Small to Mid-Sized Companies
  James C. Collins and William C. Lazier

The Contradictions That Drive Toyota's Success
  Hirotaka Takeuchi, Emi Osono and Norihiko Shimizu

The Great Game of Business
  Jack Stack

The Hunters and the Hunted
  James B. Swartz

The Leader's New Work: Building Learning Organizations
  Peter M. Senge

The Marketing Imagination
  Theodore Levitt

The One-Firm Firm Revisited
  David Maister and Jack Walker

The One to One Future: Building Relationships One Customer at a Time Don Peppers and Martha Rogers

The Seven Habits of Highly Effective People
  Stephen R. Covey

The 21 Irrefutable Laws of Leadership
  John Maxwell

Top Management Strategy
  Benjamin B. Tregoe and John W. Zimmerman

12 Seeds for Successful Relationships
  Norm Andersen

What Can America Make?
  Jyoti Thottam

What Makes a Leader?
  Daniel Goleman

Wooden on Leadership
  John Wooden

On-Line Resources . . .

MindTools.com *Wheel of Life*, London, UK………….www.mindtools.com

Strategic Planning Tools by PlanWare……………………www.planware.org

MBTI and Strong Interest Inventory   …………..www.personalitydesk.com

Author's Bio

Linc is the retired COO of a unique manufacturing company specializing in small volume, custom products. In that capacity, he was the architect of an innovative customer-intimate, technical approach to serving the market's needs for custom designed, quick turn products. Under his "servant" leadership, the company experienced a phenomenal growth in both customers and products. He also developed a unique "team" approach that not only improved employee efficiency and morale, but also increased the company's over-all efficiency and profits.

Linc Duncanson

Areas of expertise:
- ✓ 35 Years of Experience in the Manufacturing Sector
- ✓ Systematic Marketing
- ✓ Customer Satisfaction Measurement
- ✓ Quick Turn Manufacturing Systems
- ✓ ISO 9000 Quality Systems
- ✓ Performance Management Practices
- ✓ Management Team Development
- ✓ Career Path Development Programs
- ✓ Company Communications
- ✓ Servant Leadership
- ✓ Company Values

Linc is an Eagle Scout and a Business Administration graduate from the University of Minnesota. He and his wife Ellen have four children and seven grandchildren. His current activities include teaching, mentoring, and providing consulting for small business owners in Wisconsin's St. Croix Valley. Linc's hobbies are golfing, fishing, hunting, and all family activities.

The End